love, me

A Daughter's Journey Through Loss, Loneliness and Love

Shannon Hogan Cohen

with Therapeutic Insights by
Tristen Vance Henderson

Love, Me: A Daughter's Journey Through Loss, Loneliness and Love
Published by Deckle Way Press
Del Mar, California, U.S.A.

Deckle Way Press
1155 Camino Del Mar, Suite 116
Del Mar, CA 92014

HOGAN COHEN, SHANNON, Author
LOVE, ME
SHANNON HOGAN COHEN

Therapeutic Insights by Tristen Vance Henderson, LMFT

This book contains reflections based on true events as experienced and understood by the author from childhood into adulthood. While every effort has been made to remain true to the spirit of those experiences, memory is inherently subjective. These entries reflect the author's perceptions and emotions at the time they were written and are not intended as objective accounts or judgments. Some individuals may be portrayed in ways they do not recognize or agree with. These portrayals are not meant to cause harm, assign blame, or define character but rather to represent the perspective of a child navigating complex circumstances. Readers are encouraged to view these entries as personal reflections, not absolute truths. Names and identifying details may have been changed or omitted to protect privacy.

ISBN: 979-8-9913234-0-6, 979-8-9913234-2-0 (paperback)
ISBN: 979-8-9913234-3-7 (hardcover)
ISBN: 979-8-9913234-1-3 (digital)

Library of Congress Control Number: 2025911910

PSYCHOLOGY / Grief & Loss
BIOGRAPHY & AUTOBIOGRAPHY / Women
LITERARY COLLECTIONS / Letters
FAMILY & RELATIONSHIPS / Death, Grief, Bereavement

Cover Design: Julie Kuris, designerability.au
Interior Layout: Amit Dey, amitdey2528@gmail.com
Publishing Management: Susie Schaefer, finishthebookpublishing.com

QUANTITY PURCHASES: Schools, companies, professional groups,
clubs, and other organizations may qualify for special terms
when ordering quantities of this title.
For information, please visit www.shannonhogancohen.com

DECKLE WAY PRESS

Dedication

For my father,
who left too soon but never really left me.
And for the little girl with the pen in her hand—
you kept writing, even when it hurt.

For anyone who has loved and lost,
may these pages remind you:
you are not alone. Your story matters.

Introduction

Dear Reader,

For my entire life, I wore an identity that wasn't entirely my own. It was an identity shaped by the relentless need to please and prop up those around me—my mother, who lacked the courage to defend herself against domineering men; my sister, whom I had to mother and felt responsible for; and my husband, who remained loyal to a narcissistic father and struggled to stand up for our shared injustices. This facade of people-pleasing was a survival mechanism, but it came at the cost of my true self.

My journey with grief began early, at the tender age of eleven, when I lost my dad. His absence left a void that I tried to fill by being everything to everyone, hoping to protect and support those I loved in the ways I couldn't protect myself from the overwhelming loss. This grief shaped my identity and my actions for decades, intertwining with my need to please and serve.

The moment I realized how much of my life had been spent catering to others was both devastating and liberating. The old version of me, built on the shaky foundation of others' expectations and needs, died that day. In its place, a new self-began to emerge—a self that embarked on a life review, piecing together past diary entries and present reflections to make sense of my story.

As I embarked on this journey of self-discovery, I also made a vow to protect my two sons from repeating the generational mistakes that had plagued our family. This book is not only a testament to my resilience and transformation but also a guide to breaking free from the cycles of the past.

This is the story, or rather a kind of "life review," uncovering who I truly am and who I want to be, free from the burdens of people-pleasing, overaccommodating, and harmony-chasing, ensuring that my sons have the strength to forge their own paths without the weight of inherited patterns. It is a journey through grief, loss, and ultimately, profound personal growth.

As I sit in my office holding a glossy print in my hand with a faded façade, I'm desperate to connect the present with the past. The surface of the photo is smooth but with noticeable imperfections—a tiny tear and crease exist but the nostalgic feel of the image lingers. The picture exudes a sense of simplicity and innocence—the sweet face of a girl in her first-grade school picture.

My heart fills with great love and empathy for her as I look at those big brown eyes. A shy smile and gentle expression hide the fire within her soul. Her brown hair, cut in a classic bowl style, is shiny and straight. A plaid shirt peeks at the collar and hem of her cozy maroon sweater.

I pause, holding her in my thoughts and my heart.

At fifty, I am that same girl but now with wavy brown hair, thanks to hormonal changes, and a button nose which holds up one of my twenty-two pairs of readers randomly placed throughout my home. My eyes are still warm and inviting, but now more expressive and framed by fine lines that tell stories of a life well-lived that comes with age and experience.

Tapping into who we are and what we want from life is no easy undertaking. This vision of myself entering the first grade, not yet knowing grief, is empowering. It reminds me of who I was at that age—ripples of fearlessness were beginning to bubble within me.

Reacquainting myself with that little girl encouraged me to return to my eleven-year-old self, to my girlhood, to where I am today, and where I want to be moving forward.

I am thankful for Tristen, trusted therapist turned friend and comrade, who has guided me with invaluable benefits—a profound insight into my behaviors, emotions, and thought patterns throughout the fifteen years of my healing journey. Through Tristen's guidance, I have identified the root causes of my struggles and understand the impact of my past experiences on my present self. This clarity has been crucial in fostering self-awareness and personal growth. Tristen has been a constant source of support and validation. In the safe space of therapy, I have been able to express my feelings and process my emotions without judgment.

My mom did take me to a therapist I dubbed "Boring Bruce," but I did not have the emotional skills to articulate my feelings and his skills in communicating with children were limited.

It wasn't until later, in my thirties, that I found myself sitting in a therapy office with a spirited intern who was finishing her hours to obtain her Marriage Family Therapy license. I felt fortunate that the universe connected Tristen and me, as I had attempted several other counselors. I appreciated Tristen's no-nonsense approach to problems, her tendency to swear like a truck driver, and her introduction to "narcissistic behavior" after I shared a short situation about my father-in-law. My husband's father had a way of making me feel like my feelings about "his behavior" were my fault. Manipulative behavior can do that.

Little did I know she would be instrumental in creating an essential safe space for me to unpack my past, allowing me to confront and work through traumas and challenges with compassion and understanding. We all need a little help getting through this thing we call life. Far too often, I found that when I was in the worst part of my struggle, I was relying too much on myself to get me out of the vortex. No one around me could relate; they were not doing the work. However, with Tristen's input, together with my journaling and breaking down powerful and fundamental truths that I needed to accept about other people for me to live a better life, I finally began to see the bigger picture of how I was enabling and part of the problem.

I wasted too much time, energy, and attention trying to control people and situations.

Tristen helped me step back and see my need to control everything is a trauma response.

I spent many years living in a heightened state of alertness, constantly looking for potential threats, and boy, did they ever keep coming. My hypervigilance could be translated into the need to control my surroundings to avoid perceived danger.

Is this learned behavior? Absolutely.

I am still in the process of unlearning it and recognize my responses were coping mechanisms that worked in those chaotic and unstable environments that I grew up in.

Therefore, this comeback is personal. It is like an apology to myself for putting up with far too many years of destructive and deviant behavior of those close to me, including myself. Was I falling apart, I asked myself, or was I coming back together? All my experiences and perspectives did get shattered, but they were teachable moments that allowed me to love myself again, in complete form, not just the crumbs from what I was giving others.

Walking the healing path alone has been lonely, but I know it is mandatory. Observing and accepting have been my biggest challenges as I live with this new version of myself. For far too long, I would chase people to get them to see me or accept me, trying to ignore what they were showing me, and all while I should have let them be and not tried to settle for their behaviors when I knew deep down we were not in alignment.

My journey is one of pain, loneliness, and grief. But also one of hope, love, and healing. Learning to love and respect myself hasn't been easy, but it has been worth it. My greatest hope is that by joining me in revisiting my story, you will find a way to redefine yours and learn to love yourself a little bit more, too.

love, me

PART I

The Grieving Years

Dear Reader,

Everything changed the day my dad died. I don't just mean that I no longer had a dad. I mean, *everything* changed. My mom. My grandma. My sister. My life.

When I close my eyes and think of my dad, I try to remember how much fun we had when he would take me camping, riding on our four-wheelers, or being together. Dad understood me. We used to laugh and talk all the time.

Now that he's gone, I don't know how to laugh, and nobody wants to talk to me. At least not about the things that Dad talked to me about.

Mom acts like nothing changed, and Grandma doesn't seem to know how to act sometimes. I don't know if it's because they aren't sad or because they are too sad.

Dad hated peas, and so do I. Mom gets mad when she sees me picking them out, so I try to hide them in my napkin, but she figured that out. Now she makes me keep my napkin on my lap. She says that's the proper way anyway.

I don't care about proper. I care about how I hate peas and how Mom never talks to me. I care about how sad I am, but I'm even more concerned about how nobody wants to talk to me about it. I care that the last time I saw my dad, he was in a casket wearing a suit that he would have hated and looking like someone else. I worry that my life will never be the same.

Since Mom won't talk to me, I pulled out an old notebook one night. I know it doesn't make sense, but I decided to write to Dad to tell him how I'm feeling.

At least then someone will know what I'm going through.

*   *   *

So, here I am, diving in to share what lies at the heart and soul of it all: a sweet little girl with a bowl cut and maroon sweater, whose smile has shifted – at times to sadness, anger and bewilderment – as she tries to make sense of an increasingly caustic and chaotic world from age eleven to fifty.

Buckle up, it's a journey.

Now, a quick note about what you'll find here: I'm blending diary entries from my younger years with a few therapy sessions with Tristen sprinkled in for good measure. It's a pretty straightforward formula. The idea is to reflect on how those raw moments of my life link to the bigger picture. I hope it encourages you to think about your own story and how, despite our unique characters and plot twists, we're all working through the same universal themes.

And for those who may not always be portrayed in the most flattering light, please know this isn't a hit piece! The goal isn't character assassination but to give an honest account of how you made me feel in those moments. Trust me, I'm just sticking to the truth as I saw it— stripped down and without a filter, as always.

love, me

September 1985–September 1987
Eleven to Thirteen Years Old

Dear Dad,

My life sucks without you in it. Nobody understands me like you did.

I miss you so much. I need someone to talk to, even though you can't answer back.

Mom is busy. Shiloh's just a kid. The only one who gets it is Grandma Hogan. But she isn't you.

I'm back in school, but my friends act weird around me now.

Mom sold my four-wheeler. I told her not to, but nobody seems to care what I think. Who would take me riding anyway? You were the only one who liked doing that.

I'm going to always remember that you liked taking me on the four-wheeler. And that you liked to tell stories around the campfire when we were up north together. I'm never going to forget that.

I'm in my room right now. I'm on my bed writing with that colored pencil you liked. The one with all the colors stacked up so you don't have to have a bunch of different pencils. I always thought it was funny that your favorite color was yellow. It's so hard to see it on paper. I'm using purple because I used up all the black drawing pictures of us on the four-wheeler. If you were here, you could probably fix it so I could still use black. I asked Mom, but she wouldn't even try.

She has the TV turned up too loud. I can hear it even with my door closed. There's another storm coming, but I am not afraid. Remember when you used to say that the rain made you feel calm? It does that for me now, too, even though I feel like I have a storm inside of me. I'm mad that you died. Not at you. Not really.

Sometimes I want to scream, but I know that won't bring you back. I now have to rely on myself since you are gone.

I did all the right things. I made my bed and didn't talk back even though I wanted to, because so much of what grown-ups say doesn't make sense. I don't swear or lie.

It isn't fair that God took you away. You were too young to die, and you had me and Shiloh to take care of.

I am really angry right now. A better word is livid. I spelled that correctly in last year's Spelling Bee with Mr. Keup. I like using big words. It makes me feel grown up, and since everyone treats me like a grown-up, I had better start acting like one.

The teachers at Trinity Lutheran Church and School (and Mom!) keep saying that we all need to give grace to those who don't deserve it. I'm supposed to forgive people—even those mean girls from the Catholic school who pulled my hood and pushed me down on the sidewalk. But, Dad, showing mercy to others has been hard.

Mom told me you didn't even believe in God until you got sick and started reading the Bible. I hope you found a way to believe in Heaven, though I don't think it would be better than being here with me.

I miss you, and even though you can't talk to me anymore, I feel better when I still think about you. I don't think Mom would understand that, so I'm not telling her or anyone else that I'm writing to you. It can be our secret.

I hope that you can hear me and help me. I know you probably can't, but I keep telling myself you can.

This will make me feel better.

love, me

Dear Dad,

I was thinking about you today and realized that I can't remember your voice. I close my eyes and try, but all I can hear in my head is jumbled words that don't make sense. I wish I had a recording of you talking.

Sometimes, I close my eyes and think as hard as I can, but I think I'm starting to forget you.

One thing I do remember is that Mom always told you to answer the phone correctly. Instead of saying "hello," you always said, "yeah." Mom hated it, but I thought it was cool that you did the opposite of what everyone else did. I loved that. I think about that every time the phone rings, and it still makes me laugh.

I wish you were here. I've been feeling really alone lately. There is so much I want to share with you. I can't tell other people the stuff I used to say to you. They all want to pretend like you didn't die, and I can't do that. That makes me feel left out a lot.

I cried myself to sleep last night. I do that a lot now, but I shove my head in my pillow to make sure no one hears me. I don't want Mom to know. She still doesn't ever cry. Sometimes I think she doesn't miss you. She doesn't talk about feelings or you!

You were the one person I looked up to all my life. I might only be eleven, but even I know you were the one who was teaching me about life.

I want my words to grow wings and visit you in heaven so that you can find a way to send words back to me, too.

love, me

Dear Dad,

The car ride with Mom today felt routine, but the place we were going to did not.

Clouds were moving in as we drove. My window was down, and the air outside smelled like rain. That didn't bother me. I have always loved storms!

Mom's favorite radio station was playing. It isn't my favorite, but they did play "Come Sail Away" by Styx. You really liked their music. I do, too. It's funny how a song can make you feel close to someone even when they aren't there. It made me wish I was riding with you in your truck with all the windows down.

Lately, Mom and I seem off when we are together. I want to talk to her about you, but I don't know how, and about your death, but she never asks me. Maybe I should start the conversation, but again, I don't know where to begin.

When Mom pulled up to this building, I begged her not to make me go in. She said that I would be fine and that it would be good for me. She didn't seem to care about how scared I was.

I really don't think she has any idea of what is actually good for me because she never talks to me or asks me anything about how I am. We have never talked about your death. I wished you were there with me. That's dumb to even say 'cause if you were there then I wouldn't need to be.

It was raining so hard by the time we got out of the car that Mom and I were both drenched when we reached the lobby of the old building. It reeked like Gram's basement, like wet dog and old shoes. Then Mom dropped me off at one of the offices inside and told me to use my manners.

I'm tired of hearing Mom tell me that. I don't feel like using my manners. I overheard Gram tell Mom I have a "back-talking problem." Maybe I do sometimes but that's because Mom never listens and only does what she wants. Did you think I talked back too much?

Mom left me at this super small and messy office which was more like a den where wild animals might hide. I was more annoyed than amazed, but I'm really more mad at her for leaving me there. I noticed a torn *National Geographic* with a green-eyed girl on the cover sitting on a table. Before I could pick it up, an odd-looking man appeared in the doorway and asked me to follow him to his office.

I kind of felt like time just slowed down. Why do I have to go to therapy? Did you ever go to therapy? Am I the only one who needs help to talk about times when I feel sad?

If my friends knew I was there, they would make fun of me for being different. They already think I'm different because you died. This would just make it worse.

Why doesn't Mom need to go talk to a doctor? She isn't doing any better than I am. She just pretends like nothing has changed. It's like she doesn't care that you are dead.

I thought about where she might be right then. I pictured her going to the IGA to buy ring bologna for dinner and a six-pack of Diet Vernors.

I sat down on a big chair with odd-shaped stains that seemed to match my mood—uncomfortable and unhappy. Though not as uncomfortable and unhappy as the fish swimming in the dirty tank this guy had in his office. I bet that those fish were also wishing to be somewhere else— anywhere, besides there!

Then, this odd-looking man came in to talk to me. He told me his name was Bruce. He was wearing a brown three-button sweater that reminded me of Mr. Rogers. He probably thought that made him look nice and friendly. I thought he looked stupid and rumpled, like his office. There was stuff everywhere.

After what seemed like forever, Bruce asked me, "Why do you think you are here, Shannon?"

I just stared at his dirty fish tank and ignored him.

Do they teach all therapists to ask the same silly questions? I grabbed this tattered pillow he had on the chair I was sitting in and squeezed it. So much was going through my head.

Like how much I didn't like that guy. He seemed boring and had no personality. He probably ate Twinkies for dinner! That thought kind of made me giggle inside which made me feel a little less nervous.

I still didn't want to talk to him about my feelings. Besides, Bruce knew why I was there. Mom told him. I heard her tell this guy named Bill, too.

Bill is a social worker she talked to about me. She told him, "My daughter is almost twelve years old, and her father died of cancer. He was thirty years old. I don't know how to help her."

This happened right after you died when she took me to this Visiting Nurse's place, where this Bill made me and four other kids draw pictures with crayons. He asked for pictures of my happiest time with you.

I had a ton of "happiest times" with you, Dad.

I liked watching you hit golf balls at the driving range. The first time I sent my ball soaring was awesome. I remember thinking, *If Dad can do it, so can I.*

I drew my absolute favorite memory of us: two four-wheelers on a sand dune with two smiling faces.

If I close my eyes, I can still see you grinning at me, next to Uncle Tim on your orange Suzuki 225—who looked totally terrified or freaked out— while I scaled that steep dune with my orange Suzuki 125 and was side-by-side with the two of you. Yes, you told me to stay at the base of the dune with cousin Tim John and wait until you returned. But, I had overheard you and Uncle Tim talking about sand particles constantly moving, making it harder on those sheer slopes. The Bo Gap dune was a doozy. You told me it was named for the depth of its slope and vertical ascent. And I knew I could make it up that dune too!

I can still see it.

It was dusk, and our headlights were on. We all watched Uncle Tim flip his red three-wheeler, attempting to make the climb. A voice in my head urged me, "You've got this, Shannon! Just go for it!"

Tim John yelled, "Don't go! You'll get in trouble." I can still hear it.

I ignored him and took off anyway. It was so exciting to make my way up that sand dune without slipping or tipping over. I was nine, almost ten, and I thought I could do anything. You were full of pride in me, too. Right then and there, I knew I would never stop wanting to make you proud!

I was thinking all these thoughts, when I heard Boring Bruce asking me how your passing makes me feel.

So dumb, right?

Like I would feel anything but horrible.

Who feels good after their dad dies?

I figured I needed to reconsider my approach with these annoying therapists. I thought that maybe if I talked a little more, they might leave me alone. I stared out the window for a while and watched the rain drip down the dirty pane. I pretended to be okay, but I felt like my heart was crying inside me. Then I just blurted out that I *obviously* missed you because you were my everything.

I hoped Bruce got the message, an obvious answer to a stupid question should make him feel dumb for being so dumb. I wanted to hit the pillow as hard as I could.

I don't know how to talk about the pain I'm feeling with people I don't know. I should be talking to Mom about this, but like I said, she doesn't want to hear me.

Mom says therapy is for my "betterment," but it feels more like a punishment. There was no way that I would tell this guy anything about my feelings. He doesn't have any right to know how I feel about you. I don't know him, and I don't trust him.

How are you supposed to talk to a stranger about something so personal? It doesn't seem right.

I got a little sassy, to be honest. When Boring Bruce asked how I felt talking to him, I told him that not being there with him would make me happy. I kind of felt bad for him when I said that but I also kind of felt like it needed to be said. It was the truth, after all.

I couldn't sit there and be silent because I knew Mom was paying Bruce money to talk to me and you and Mom always taught us not to be careless with time and money.

I still get in trouble for leaving the lights on in my room. And you always told me to be nice to people, even if I don't like them. I guess this goon counted.

Life feels harder since you died. There is this painful gap between who I thought I was and the person I'm being forced to be now.

Unlike social worker Bill, who asked me to draw something happy, Boring Bruce asked me to draw something that made me feel sad. I scribbled for a minute and handed over a sloppy sketch. When he asked me what it was that I had drawn, I told him it was oyster stew.

Remember how every Christmas Eve we had to eat that bowl of milky mud that Great-Grampie made? It always smelled like barf. I wonder if Bruce understood what my drawing was saying: *I don't like you, and I don't like oyster stew.*

Being there was not my choice. Boring Bruce started getting annoyed with me as time went on, but I really didn't care. I wanted to annoy him! I wonder if this is how you felt when Mom would remind you daily to answer the phone correctly.

Annoying Boring Bruce made a small part of me happy. He even looked sort of angry, like Mom did when you wouldn't listen to her.

When it was finally time for me to go and Mom came to pick me up, she made me shake this man's hand. I didn't want to, but I did so that we could leave.

I felt safe being back inside Mom's car. Simon and Garfunkel's song, "The Sound of Silence," played on the radio as we drove home. That was weirdly appropriate. It seems like there's always silence between me and Mom now. She didn't ask me anything about my time with Boring Bruce. It kind of made me mad so I decided to stay silent, too.

I don't understand why Mom won't talk to me. Doesn't she care how I feel? Why did she make me sit in some creepy play-pen with some strange therapist? Boring Bruce doesn't even care enough to take care of his fish, why would he care about me?

If Mom wants us to get along better and improve my "tough behavior," maybe she should talk to me herself. I don't know what to do, Dad. If you were here, I bet you could make her listen.

It took us longer to get home today because of the thunderstorm, but that didn't matter to me. I didn't mind being alone with my thoughts. I only wish you were here. When we got home, I went downstairs and rollerskated in the basement to music. "Karma Chameleon" is my favorite song. I never really understood what it meant, but Cousin Poppy told me it was about not being afraid to be who you are. I think that's what I loved most about you, you didn't care what others thought. You just were who you were. I don't know what I'll be when I get older, but I'd like to think I'll be like you.

One thing I do know for sure is that I'm not going to ever go see those fish again.

love, me

Dear Dad,

With Mom working as a beautician from our home, there are always little old ladies visiting her basement salon.

I'm not sure how Mom stays in there so long. Between the smell of perm solution and the homemade sauerkraut we have stored in those chipped crocks, it can get pretty smelly. Sometimes, I get queasy from breathing all that in…and also from going up and down and spinning around in Mom's salon chair.

I put up with the smells just to ride that thing. You always encouraged me to go faster when Mom said to stop. That made me smile. But, as good as that chair is, I still think the hairdryer chair is my very favorite! Sitting under the hooded dryer with a head full of perm rods, eating a frozen turkey meal for dinner is one of my favorite things to do. That might sound funny, but I love those dinners, and the dryer feels good and drowns out all the noise around me, including in my head. It's like an escape.

When I'm in the basement, I overhear a lot of conversations Mom has with her customers. These ladies… and some men, too… tell Mom a lot when they're sitting in her cushy yellow chair. Maybe that is why Mom doesn't want to talk to me. Maybe she is all talked out after chatting with her clients.

Did she talk to you a lot? Or did she just yell at you for all the things she thought you did wrong?

love, me

Dear Dad,

Today, a lanky-looking woman was waiting for us as we pulled into the driveway. She was not one of Mom's regular customers, but a friend from her group of gal pals who play cards and eat odd things once a month.

The club was at our house last night and Mom made that creamy white dip of hers that has chipped beef in it. I can't remember if you liked it, but I think it's the bomb! I snuck a scoop onto a potato chip. It was worth getting yelled at in front of all her gal pals.

Anyway, I'm not sure if Mom expected this lady to stop today but she seemed happy to see her. While she chatted with her outside, I was told to take the groceries in and set the table for dinner. I think the lady's name is Delores. Did you know her? I think Mom was probably telling her about how I misbehaved at Boring Bruce's office.

Unpacking the groceries, I saw Mom got all the stuff to make tuna noodle casserole for dinner. I like that dinner, except for the peas she always wants to add to it. I hate peas, just like you did. The dish is much better without them. Since Mom was outside, I hid the can of peas I unpacked in the pantry, hoping she wouldn't notice them missing. I bet you would have done the same! I wonder why we can't have the yummy things Mom makes for her club ladies for our dinner.

I wonder if you miss our house and Evie and Viola. They are still my favorite neighbors.

Viola still drinks her Earl Grey tea from that same dainty cup. Two weeks after you died, she let me snoop around her cluttered garage and pick out some treasures to take home. I was kind of surprised that Mom allowed me to keep them. One of the things I found that I really like is an aqua-green mason jar. I got rid of the rusty lid and now the jar is on my desk, holding my favorite sparkly markers.

You'd be happy to know that Evie is still the same. She still likes to drink beer and she still likes to have fun. She reminds me of you sometimes— both mischief-makers who always had plenty of tricks to play on one another.

I kind of feel you near me when I'm with Evie but, even so, it's not the same anymore. I miss all the times I sat with her on her tiny porch waiting for you to walk home from work.

Her feet still dangle off her favorite blue and white webbed folding chair because she is so short, but we don't play the game we did before. I used to love that game. It made the time we waited for you so much fun. We'd sit there and try to guess the color of the next car to come down North Street, until we'd see you round the corner.

It's kind of hard to sit on her porch now, especially if it's at the end of the day. I just want to see you coming down the street.

I loved how you walked so fast in those brown-laced shoes you always wore. As you got nearer, I could see your smile and I'd start waving at you like crazy.

I wonder if Evie misses you. I think I will ask her tomorrow. Or maybe not. I wonder if it makes Mom mad when I talk about you. She never does, but I don't want Evie to get mad and Mom to tell her I can't visit anymore.

I just want you to come back. Then everything would be like it was before... happy, fun and... normal.

love, me

Dear Dad,

Mom is very busy.

Lately, she has been leaving me home with Shiloh a lot. Sometimes, it bothers me, but since I'm the one in charge, I don't have to answer to anyone else.

Terry still runs over from next door to check on us sometimes, but I can take care of my sister.

I don't know if Mom really appreciates my help. She gets to go off for the weekend and never thanks me for taking care of things. The only time she gives me any attention is when I'm in trouble— which seems to happen more now than when you were here.

We always seemed to be in some sort of trouble together. It was easier to have a sidekick to get in trouble with. One of my favorite memories is when you lit up all those bottle rockets in the backyard. Mom and Evie were upset about those fireworks, but you never seemed bothered about other people's reactions. You did what made you happy.

I want to do the same.

I love riding my bike to see Grandma Rosie. Maybe because she's your mom, I feel like she is the closest person to you, other than me. It's pretty easy for me to get to her duplex since it's only four miles from our house.

A few weeks ago, I overheard Grandma Rosie's older sister getting her hair done in the basement and telling Mom that she admired the way Grandma forged on.

"Life didn't stop and mourn with her," she said. When I heard Aunt Deke say that I thought about how Grandma Rosie lost her mom, husband, and son all within three years.

I don't know if she talked to anyone about being sad, maybe not. Whether she did or not, I sometimes wonder if her feelings feel trapped inside the way mine do. Maybe I could talk to Grandma on my next visit?

Was she a good listener when you were growing up?

I think she is a rebel in many ways. Like Bo and Luke on *Dukes of Hazzard*, she follows her own rules—maybe that's where you learned to do that.

Grandma never seems lonely living alone. None of her losses seem to affect her. Maybe she can teach me her tricks. I think I might ride my bike to her house after lunch. Since it's Saturday, I will stop at the Dairy Barn for my favorite drippy, soft-served ice cream cone dipped in chocolate. I know if you were here, you'd have one with me.

Mom still doesn't eat ice cream. She'd never share a bowl of vanilla ice cream with me, like you used to do. Do you remember that plastic tub with the orange handle? I used to love it when you'd drizzle chocolate syrup on it and then swirl it all together. It was the creamiest concoction I had ever tasted.

You and Mom seemed like opposites to me.

Mom doesn't like drawing attention to herself.

You were different.

People liked you, Dad.

But nobody liked you more than me. I feel like I'm starting to do better, but then something happens, and I want to tell you about it. Then I remember you are gone and I'm sad all over again. I hope this feels better soon. I don't want to miss you like this forever.

love, me

Dear Dad,

Now that you are gone, Mom makes me take Shiloh with me everywhere. It's so annoying!

I liked being the only child and grandchild in our family for seven years. I never wanted to share you or my stuff with anyone else. Being an only child was fun.

I remember when you came home from the hospital with baby Shiloh. You had her tiny footprints stamped on your right bicep in black ink. Her footprints were so small they looked like they could have been made by my Cabbage Patch doll, Annette.

I can still see the smile you had on your face that day. You were so proud when you got home with Shiloh.

I remember looking at little feet on your arm and thinking about how different it would be with another person in our house. But, honestly, after Shiloh was born, my world didn't really change that much. You and I still spent a lot of time alone together. Sometimes, I think we hung out more after Shiloh was born since Mom was always busy taking care of her and working.

Remember how Shiloh cried a lot when she first came home... and still kind of does.

Even now, she still has those same rosy, red cheeks. You had a way with her, though. I remember all the silly faces you made. She loved that. I think she misses you, too.

I don't think I was ever jealous of Shiloh and the attention she got when she first came home from the hospital, though I thought it was weird when all the relatives wanted to hold her. I felt like I should be the one to get to hold her since she was my sister, but everyone always thought I would drop her because she was so wiggly. I liked that you let me when no one else did. You were so patient in showing me how and telling me that I always had to make sure to hold her head.

Mom always made her smell like baby powder.

Even though I've grown to love Shiloh and like having a little sister, we are still a whole seven years apart. We just do different things.

She still watches a lot of television. Television is boring to me. I sometimes wish I could lay on the floor under a blanket with my head on a pillow like she does and just chill. But, for some reason, I can't.

I like to have silly fun, like you and I always did. This sometimes gets me in trouble, like when I hop on the back of Shiloh's rusty red tricycle and use my feet to make her go faster. She always ends up crying and running back inside the house to tell Mom on me.

It makes it hard to see my friends when she's always tagging along. It's not Shiloh's fault, but it sometimes makes me mad. It's not fair and is just one more thing that makes me wish you were still here.

love, me

Dear Dad,

I still try to go to Grandma Rosie's house every week. I like being close to her. It makes me feel close to you.

When I first learned to ride my bike, you would hold on to the back of my floral banana seat, trying to steady me while I steered along the sidewalk. I hope teaching me to ride that heavy purple bike when I was just five is a fun memory for you, too.

I feel like you were always teaching me things. You taught me what a flooded engine was and how to pull-start my four-wheeler when I was nine. I will never forget your face lighting up with pride, just like when you set off those firecrackers in the backyard.

Today, I went to the backyard and sprawled on the wet grass near my old sandbox. I missed you today more than usual, though I am not sure how that is even possible.

Looking up at the big blue sky scattered with those cotton ball clouds relaxed me. Maybe it's just being outside, smelling the fresh cut grass, and hearing the birds chirping that made me feel better. You used to love all those things, too.

Laying there made me feel comfortable being alone with my thoughts, happily watching the robins land on our clothesline. I thought for a minute that maybe one of them might have been you, trying to tell me everything will be okay.

Were you one of those robins today, Dad?

love, me

Dear Dad,

My trusty, purple bike got me all the way to Grandma Rosie's house really fast today.

Most people slow down when they see railroad tracks, but not me. As long as I don't see or hear the train, I speed up. Don't be mad. I like the thrill. The lights aren't flashing, so I know the train isn't coming. But the gaps worry me a little, I don't want my bike tire to get stuck.

When I rode up to Grandma's, I waved at her neighbor, Dorothy. I think they are close in age, but Grandma looks younger to me. Sometimes, the three of us watch this new show called *Golden Girls* together at Dorothy's house and eat the yummy brownies she bakes for us. We laugh at the silly things those four women do.

I like all the characters, but my favorite is Sophia. She's a tiny, spunky, white-haired lady. Like Grandma, she seems to be a straight talker and a good cook. Dorothy acts the same as all the other adults in my life... she never talks about your death so whenever she is at Grandma's I don't get to ask questions about you or tell her how I'm feeling.

Why is that? Do grown-ups not know how to talk about feelings? I know I don't, but I'm only eleven. You'd think that by the time you get to Mom's age or older you'd be better at being able to talk about feelings.

I hope I am.

love, me

Dear Dad,

Grandma's house always feels warm and inviting. It's kind of become my sanctuary, even more than church. She still hasn't fixed the screen door. She tried putting WD-40 on it, but it still squeaks.

When I got there yesterday, there was a jar of her slippery, sweet peaches sitting on the table. That made me smile because we used to get in trouble for eating an entire jar without sharing.

Grandma and I spend hours sprawled out on her carpet coloring. My pages never look as good as hers. I use the sharpener in the back of the box, thinking this will make a difference in my coloring, but it never does.

Grandma's finished pages always look like an artist's work. She always picks the best colors and never gets outside the lines. She says, "It takes time to get this good."

When I got bored with coloring, we played Old Maid and Gin Rummy. Grandma laughs every time I get the ornery-looking Old Maid, and she barely gets it for some reason.

Do you think she cheats?

Sometimes I think maybe she does, but then I know in my heart she would never do that to me.

I do get her back with my sequences in Gin Rummy.

We never gamble for anything. So, you don't need to worry about me developing bad habits. It's more about neither of us wanting to lose something to the other.

You were pretty competitive, too, right?

I thought you might want to know our routine is still the same, only we don't wait for you on the porch anymore. That's the only sad part of visiting Grandma.

After hours of cards or coloring, we still drive five minutes to Main Street and pick up a medium, greasy brown box from Pompeii Pizza.

Grandma lets me have the last slice.

Was she this much fun with you growing up?

Then, after pizza, like usual, we listen to Ernie Harwell on the radio, broadcasting the play-by-play the Detroit Tigers. They are still our favorite team. I love lining up all my baseball cards on the living room carpet. I still remember when they won the 1984 World Series!

That day, you, Grandma, and I went out to her front yard and played whiffle ball. I was Lance Parish, as always, and she was Alan Trammel. You didn't play that day because you were feeling pretty sick. You sat in the lawn chair. I think you pretended to be Sparky Anderson, the coach.

Shiloh was there, too, chasing the balls.

I wish I could live with Grandma now that you are gone. I know Mom would never let me, but I feel like you would.

love, me

Dear Dad,

I know I keep writing a lot about Grandma, but going to her house makes me happy.

One of my favorite things to do with her is to walk to the Ben Franklin near the IGA where you used to work. It makes me sad sometimes, but I don't let myself cry to where Grandma would see my tears because then I may not get to pick out books.

I really like getting books.

The last time we went to the Ben Franklin, I picked out a Peter Pan book. Whenever I read that book, I imagine myself as the free-spirited young boy who flies everywhere and never grows up. I guess that's what is so great about books. They allow you to be someone other than you.

Being with Grandma is easy and that's saying a lot because I don't feel like it's easy being with anyone anymore.

Even though I'm twelve, I like to snuggle with her in her flowery crocheted afghan. She makes me feel safe and understood. She listened when I told her about Boring Bruce and how Mom made me speak to him. She's a good listener. I want to be like that when I get older.

And Grandma is clever. Sometimes she picks out stories for me to read that have relationships in them that suddenly end. I guess it's her way of trying to help me by showing me how others have had to deal with loss.

I also showed Grandma the pictures I drew with Social Worker Bill. When I did that, her eyes suddenly seemed different, and I asked her why they looked watery. She said she had blocked tear ducts. I had never heard of having blocked tears, but I could relate.

Sometimes, my eyes kind of get watery, but the tears don't come because I don't feel like I can let them. I kind of feel like this all the time, but I know I can't just start crying, like at school.

It's sometimes hard to keep that feeling bottled up, like if I do it for too long, I'm going to explode.

Grandma said nice things about the drawings I showed her. She said that I did a really good job with the faces I drew, using my fat-tipped markers. She said that the drawings I did of the two of us looked like us.

She especially liked how I drew my frizzy brown hair and your green and white Skoal hat. She even said that she liked how I used a lot of color, and that Social Worker Bill should consider using more color when he draws. I thought that was funny.

Grandma still tells me there is nothing wrong with coloring outside the lines. She says that it's okay to be different—even okay to misbehave sometimes. She reminds me a lot of you, Dad.

Sometimes, I have to share Grandma with Shiloh, but I don't mind it too much. There's always enough noodle soup for both of us.

Shiloh is still as cute as ever. She loves drinking apple juice in her pink cup and reading *The Story of Bubbles the Whale*. Grandma's copy is getting pretty worn from being read so much.

I look at that story differently now.

Bubbles and Squirt are best friends, living in the ocean, until they are suddenly separated, and Bubbles is taken to Marineland to live and perform tricks. For a long time, he was lonely for his friend but eventually got to see Squirt again.

So, the story ends happy.

Every time I read that book, I feel a little sad and a little mad, too, because I know that I'll never see you again, Dad. You and I were best buddies, just like Bubbles and Squirt.

I think I'm done writing to you for today.

Those tears I said seemed "blocked" are coming down on this paper.

I guess I was right in thinking I'd just explode. There are so many tears coming out of my eyes that I could never count all of them. It makes it hard to see.

love, me

Dear Dad,

Christmas sucks.

Mom is dating some weird guy who I named "Dorky Dude" and is almost bald. He gives me a bad feeling. I don't trust him.

Mom goes to visit him almost every weekend. He lives an hour away, so she doesn't get to see him during the week.

I stay home and take care of Shiloh when Mom is gone. I'm not really sure if we should be alone since I'm only twelve. I like being in charge, but sometimes I worry that something bad will happen and I won't know what to do. But I do like not having to answer to anyone when Mom is away. Terry and her Mom are across the street, and all the other neighbors are really close.

It's confusing, but I feel pretty confused a lot of the time now. I don't really know what I'm supposed to feel. So, I don't think about it and ignore that voice inside me.

Sometimes I just want to hang out with my friends, but it all seems so different now.

Before you died, everyone thought I was outgoing like you. I could make friends quickly and knew how to get a laugh. I fit in with the other fifth-grade kids just fine. But when you died, and I started sixth grade, and it just wasn't the same anymore.

It's just really, really hard now with my friends. They all look at me like I'm weird now. Basically, they all have dads, and I don't.

It's hard to fit in.

I'm uncomfortable and don't know how to act sometimes. Maybe they don't mean to make me feel so different, but it hurts. Their lives haven't changed and mine is upside down. I guess they don't know how to act around me sometimes either. I just know I don't like it. It makes me think I don't belong anymore.

I feel a little better when I'm playing sports. Coach Frost is always impressed by how well I can dribble a basketball. It's nice when he says I'm playing well. It helps me forget about not fitting in at school.

I learned how to dribble from all those hours we spent in the church parking lot, shooting baskets and practicing. I keep telling Coach that you taught me everything I know.

Now, I guess, Coach will be teaching me. I think you'd be okay with that since I don't think you'd want me to stop playing. But I would rather it was you.

love, me

Dear Dad,

I still keep getting the "poor Shannon looks." It comes across as pity, like they feel so sorry for me, and it makes me feel bad. It's like it separates me from everyone else as different.

As bad as the "poor Shannon looks" are, the comments I get from some of the kids at school are the most hurtful.

I won't name names, but there's a seventh-grade boy, who has super dirty fingernails, who asked me shortly after you died, "Who will cut your lawn now?"

I couldn't find the energy to holler back at him, "I will, you dimwit!" The world feels mean, and so do the people around me.

Walking home today in the snow, a bunch of girls from St. Elizabeth School ran up to me, pulled my hair, and said I looked like a boy. While running away, one shouted, "Trinity Lutheran is for losers!" I was too mad to cry on the outside, but inside, I sobbed, shivering and wishing I was wherever you are.

I wish I could feel like I did at the end of fifth grade, happy and confident. I wish everything could just go back to that time and you would still be alive.

You were the only one who really understood me.

My relationship with Mom hasn't changed. She never took time to do stuff with me or talk to me. But now, without you here, it just feels lonelier. I feel like there's a huge hollow space inside me. I want Mom to fill it but she never takes the time to talk to me for some reason. You would think she'd realize that she needs to do that now that you aren't here.

You allowed me to be different, Dad, without judgment. You made me feel like I was seen and heard.

We were silly together and that always felt good. I guess I am different from my friends. They don't have this heaviness in their hearts. They still have their dads. It seems really unfair to lose a dad and super wrong to lose one as fun as mine is, or I guess was.

love, me

Dear Dad,

Today is better, but only a little. I still have so much sadness in me.

The kids at school are still dumb and need their mouths washed out with soap, like Mom does when I talk back.

I don't like it when she uses Irish Spring soap. That green bar might smell good but it's nasty tasting. I prefer Coast.

Do you remember the sixth-grade teacher at Trinity, Mrs. Bass?

She is beginning to fill a space where I want Mom to be. She is wholesome. She feels like an angelic presence in my life. Her cheeks looked like those of the three cherub figurines on her desk. I liked how she talks to our sixth-grade class. She keeps us accountable (another Spelling Bee word I got right) without yelling. Her way of teaching feels right.

When our class is in the church, I feel a sense of calm when Mrs. Bass sings and plays the organ. She makes me feel protected when she hugs me. When I started sixth grade, you had only been gone a few weeks. Having Mrs. Bass put her arms around me made me realize I had really missed that. I was craving being seen and cared for.

I feel lucky to have Mrs. Bass give me what Mom isn't.

During chapel, I often think of Mary, Jesus's mom, who seemed to have the ability to know when to be present, to shield her son from specific harm, and to love him completely. I want Mom to do the same thing. I dream of her holding me and saying, "I know you must be in pain. I am, too. We will get through this together." I sometimes think that maybe that would give me all I need to move on, to stop feeling so sad and lonely.

I really like Mrs. Bass, but I'd give up her hugs if I could get them from Mom. I don't know how to tell Mom that I need her.

What would you do if you were here? I wish you could tell me what to do right now.

Before I forget, I want to share a story with you that happened a few weeks ago. Mrs. Bass was handing back one of our first homework assignments, and at the top of mine, in red pen, she had written, *You may want to read this when alone!*

I slid the paper into my folder without anyone seeing it and took it home to read. I was afraid the extra red ink would draw attention to me. I didn't need any more pitying eyes! While I didn't want the other kids to know that Mrs. Bass was giving me extra attention, it also secretly felt good. The minute I got home, I took out the paper and saw that Mrs. Bass had written me a message under the ten lines of my scribbled religion verses.

Here is what she wrote:

Shannon, I never have had my 'talk' with you. But maybe now might be the time. My pastor told me 'way back when' that life is like a piece of embroidery work. Our sampler has many colors interweaved in our lives. The Lord finished his embroidery work when your dad was taken to Heaven with God. When that happened, your dad's thread in your life was ended. Yet his love or thread you will always remember. All the special times you were able to share. Now, down on earth all we see are the cut threads and knots, which doesn't make much sense. But you must trust that the Master Artist—God—knows what your embroidery work looks like. Occasionally, he may let us peek at it and see that everything will be okay. So, think of your dad's life as like a golden thread in your life, helping to develop your unique pattern.

I wasn't sure what all the words meant or why she wrote what she wrote to me, but the attention felt nice.

I wanted attention from Mom, and not getting it made me feel empty. Maybe getting some from Mrs. Bass was okay, even if I got hugs and special notes that the other kids didn't.

Along with my paper, Mrs. Bass attached a copy of a poem entitled, *The Weaver.*

She also added a message at the end of the poem, saying that maybe Mom would like to read *The Weaver* poem, too! And then she signed off saying that I was in her prayers and that she loved me. This made me feel so good. The part about her loving me, that is. Not the part about sharing the poem with Mom.

Maybe Mom would like to read the poem? No way. I am the one struggling here. Mom seems fine, Dad. She's dating Dorky Dude so she can't be too sad, right? She can find her own support. Mrs. Bass is mine.

I decided not to show Mom the note Mrs. Bass wrote or the poem she attached. Was that bad of me?

I will say this to you... It was the longest poem I have ever read.

The words didn't really make sense to me. I'm guessing Mrs. Bass wants me to reflect on what the poem is saying. It's kind of what I think she was trying to say in her note. I honestly don't understand it that well.

I do know that I am tired of people telling me that God has a plan. I don't like God's plan. I told him that, too.

I'm not mad at Mrs. Bass. I think it's really nice of her to think of me, even if I don't totally get her note. I'm not even mad at Mom.

I'm angry at God for taking you from me.

This whole thing made me start wondering why Mom can't write me a note. If she doesn't want to talk to me about you, she could at least write it on paper. If she told me she understood how hard this is, and that I'm not alone, I would understand.

I wouldn't feel so sad that she doesn't talk to me or hug me.

love, me

Dear Dad,

School still feels like a series of routine, yet strange, events.

My friends seem to have forgotten about your death and started treating me like they did before. I don't feel so different now, but I know I still am. I'm still super sad and mad, but at least I can fit in better at school.

Routine is boring, though. Mom has always been one to follow routine and without you, our lives have become even more repetitive (Spelling Bee word I got wrong). It's like we are living the way Mom likes to live, without any of the fun or excitement that you brought.

Nothing feels the same or right. All our dinners and gatherings with each other are boring. It's like we are all little boring robots doing the same thing every day. Get up, get dressed, go to school, come home, do homework, help with Shiloh and whatever else Mom needs, set the table, eat a boring dinner, clean up, get ready for bed, go to sleep... and then do it all over again.

I miss you so much. My sadness never seems to end. I just learned to put my sadness in a place where I can still function.

The one routine I do like is the one Grandma has. She goes to the post office every day, and she always goes while we have recess.

I wave at her white Cutlass Supreme as she drives past the school playground. Sometimes, she stops and rolls down her window.

I'll dash up to the door and hug her.

All the teachers on duty yell at me to get off the street.

I ignore them every time. This always makes my day. It's like one little bright light in all the dullness.

love, me

Dear Dad,

My loneliness and sadness just won't go away.

I am trying to learn how to ignore my pain. It's not easy.

Every time I go to the cemetery, my heart stops for a second. I don't even know how to say how I feel.

The worst experience ever was watching the funeral home people lower your casket into the ground, knowing you were in it. I lost a part of me that day, and I don't think I'm ever going to get it back.

Sometimes, Grandma and I go to the cemetery together.

Mom placed a terra cotta pot near your headstone. She filled it with green ivy and red geraniums. I like how these plants come back every year in our pots at home. They keep growing and blooming without much care and attention.

Maybe I'm like a geranium.

Grandma always brings a green plastic watering can so she can give your flowers a good soaking. I tell you about my day and how much I miss you. I'm curious if you hear me. I ask for signs; sometimes squirrels show up, so I think you can.

I have never said this to anyone, but I think about it a lot and only wrote it now for the first time...

I want to dig up your casket and pull your body out and bring you back to life.

I have never told anyone that, and I have never left your grave without crying. Grandma seems to be able to go without ever crying. That's a trick I want to learn. Maybe it's her blocked tear ducts. Or, maybe, it's just an adult thing.

I asked Mom one day about Grandma not crying, and she said, "People handle situations differently."

She told me that not everyone will feel sad or cry. She said that some people may still be in shock about what happened and are still processing their feelings.

What she said made sense. It made me think that maybe that's why I have never seen her sob. I always thought it was strange, but maybe she is in shock.

I don't feel like my emotions can be controlled. I cry inside and outside, especially when I tell stories about you.

I definitely felt like it was a shock losing you but maybe it's just different than the shock that Grandma and Mom feel.

You never were unemotional like Mom and Grandma.

I bet my sensitivity comes from you.

Dad, you never showed any unhappiness to me. I did hear anger sometimes, from my bedroom, though.

Mom did not like it when you drank.

You'd sometimes make noises when you got home late after partying with your beer buddies. You liked Budweiser beer almost as much as you liked Pepsi.

Maybe beer made you feel better when you were sad. But it made Mom mad, and I could hear you guys screaming at each other. I'd pull my sheets up over my head to drown out your voices, but sometimes I would make myself walk out and see what was happening. I was afraid to leave my bed, but I was also afraid of what might happen if I didn't check on you.

Those were not the best visions of you, Dad. Maybe Mom was right about the beer and all your partying.

Why did you drink so much?

Were you sad?

I am not sure how to feel about this.

Maybe this is hard for you to hear, Dad.

I do like how you never drank beer around me. We drank Pepsi out of glass bottles. You also ate tuna fish sandwiches on Wonder Bread with Ruffles chips and baby dill pickles.

Mom never knew all the fun times we had together.

I want to tell her, but it may make her feel sad.

I wonder if Mom would be jealous?

Maybe Mom is mad at you?

Remember how we would wrestle in the living room? I definitely don't think Mom liked that, but we had fun. You would gently pin me down and I would wiggle and squirm until I'd finally give up and say the magic password ... Acapulco.

And how we'd visit Uncle Mel at his tool and dye shop next to the train tracks every Saturday afternoon? I miss doing that.

The screeching noises and smells in Uncle Mel's shop were terrible.

I remember sitting in his quiet office, which was really the only place that didn't stink.

I could hear you and Uncle Mel laughing through the office walls.

Our last stop on those Saturdays was another favorite—McDonald's for a quarter pounder with cheese right before we'd head home for dinner. Those burgers were much better than the tuna noodle casserole we knew we had to eat when we got home!

I like to pretend I'm sitting on the flatbed of your truck, listening to "Jack and Diane" by your favorite singer, John Cougar Mellencamp.

Do you live and just not have any more adventures at some point, or does life actually go on after you've died (only in another place, like Heaven)?

I wish you could tell me.

love, me

Dear Dad,

When I got home today, I told Mom the cemetery flowers looked nice. She still has never talked to me about your death, but neither has Grandma. I'm always the one who brings it up.

Also, I am still confused about why Grandma wasn't with us when we planned your funeral. Mom made me go with her, Aunt Cathleen, and Uncle Tim. I get that they'd go with us, being that they are your two siblings, but I don't get why Grandma didn't go.

When I walked up to the front door of the funeral home, there was a sign that said *Generations of Caring*. I guessed that meant that we all end up there?

That historic-looking red brick building with its big marble pillars out front never seemed creepy until that day. I saw it every time we went to IGA, but it never seemed scary before that day.

Then I got thinking, you walked by this place every day, super weird.

You know, Rich, the funeral director? He used to go to the Daytona 500 races in Florida with Grandma CJ and her boyfriend Howard.

You were never a big Howard fan. Me either, actually.

Rich gave us a tour of the building that started in a spacious room where he said your "showing" would be held. I didn't really know what that meant.

I think Rich told Mom to invite me. He seemed nice and kept asking me how I was. None of the grownups in my life ever ask how I am. They all pretend like they can handle all of this. I think Rich must know better. I mean he is around death a lot, so he has to know how to treat people when they are sad.

Being at the funeral home made the whole thing feel even worse, as hard as that is to believe.

It's like it's already sad and then they make it even more serious, everything felt slow and its really quiet inside. I know it's not supposed to be fun, but you wouldn't have liked it either. Whatever the adults talked about would have bored you, too. You would have cracked a joke or made a goofy face to liven up the mood, like how you used to toss a pillow or a slipper at Mom when she was reading the newspaper.

It made her mad, but I laughed every time. I liked that about you, Dad. You never took anything too seriously.

Now that you are gone, I'm learning that life is actually pretty hard. Or, as you would call it, heavy.

After we toured the viewing room at the funeral home, we went into a hallway that reminded me of an episode of the *Twilight Zone*. I thought we might be going to another world or something.

We stepped into a dark display room where caskets of all different colors, shapes, and sizes were lined up, some open and some closed. They all looked fancy and even had pillows inside.

The shiny gold handles on the casket in front of me made me think of how tight I would hold onto the black grips on the four-wheeler you bought me.

I am still ticked off that Mom sold Lizzie—that's what I named my four-wheeler. I sometimes dream of driving her back to our favorite campsite and the woods where Tim John and I liked to play hide and seek. Tim John and I were very different.

He had his red Honda three-wheeler and liked Cherry Coke. I had my trusted Lizzie and liked Pepsi, like you. I started drinking root beer now.

I felt overwhelmed being at that funeral home that day, but I kept my thoughts and feelings to myself, like Mom always does.

I remember reading about how the Egyptians made elaborate tombs and my fourth-grade teacher talking about their coffins and burial ceremonies in history class.

At eleven, I never thought I would be here helping to pick a tomb to hold my father's body or watching adults stare at each other strangely while talking about you.

I wished I was with Grandma.

No, I wished I was with you, Dad, wherever you are!

I wanted to tell someone that my life felt like a scary movie.

Scary movies were not my thing.

All I wanted to do was change the channel and watch something else.

Something more like *The Dukes of Hazard*.

I thought about Daisy in her white Jeep, driving fast down the dirt road chasing her cousins, Bo and Luke. That made my heart stop racing, at least for a moment.

The grownups that went to the funeral home talked about preparation and personalization. Rich asked Mom something about any "preplanning" and mentioned some checklist.

I was sick thinking about you being in one of those boxes.

Dad, the only place you belong is behind me on my four-wheeler, heading to the hidden watering hole.

You constantly reminded me to follow the tree line. I want you to know that teaching me that those trees would be my map and prevent me from getting lost if I paid attention was really important.

My other guideposts in the woods were the crooked branches with bright-colored leaves and logs that looked like snakes laying crisscrossed or half-buried in mossy mud.

I always found my way back to our base camp.

I don't want to be mean, but Tim John did not.

I was proud of myself when it was Tim John that you and your brother had to head out to find. You always believed in me.

I can still taste the cold ham sandwiches and bubbly Pepsi we had for lunch while we were out in the woods.

I let myself think of all these good times while the adults talked about things I didn't want to hear. Then, all of a sudden, I realized they were arguing over whether to have your casket closed or open.

Your siblings reminded Mom that you would not have wanted people to see you this way.

I agreed! But I didn't say anything.

Uncle Tim said you would not have enjoyed any of this "fanfare."

You know how I love learning new words and using them, but I did not know the meaning of that word. I asked Mrs. Bass the following day. It means "fuss."

Mom was determined that the casket be open. Rich sided with Mom, which surprised me.

All I could think was, *Dad will haunt them for having the casket open!* I wished I would have said it out loud, enough for everyone to hear. You would *not* have liked having an open casket—I know it!

I wanted to tell the adults that everyone would feel sorry for you because you didn't look like yourself when you died, but those words would not come out.

The thing I remember most about seeing you in the casket was how skinny you were in an oversized blue suit that you never would have worn when you were alive. Your hair was straight and thin instead of fuzzy and permed like you would wear it.

Seeing your eyes closed makes my tear ducts leak—and your mustache was gone! I didn't understand why anyone would do that—take something away that was so much a part of someone.

I wanted to remember your tanned skin, your muscle, your moxie (another word I spelled right in the Spelling Bee), your zaniness (I got this word wrong), and your zest for life.

I didn't want to remember some lifeless body lying there like a ghost with no fuzz on your face.

The adults picked out a solid oak casket with pine trees on each corner. I did think it was the right choice. I counted the trees on the casket. There were four.

You were buried right next to a tall pine tree, just like the ones on the casket you were laid to rest in.

I know you would not like the squirrels scurrying around near that tree by your gravestone. Then again, it might make you smile knowing that the pesky hoarders are safe from your trust-worthy Remington rifle.

love, me

Dear Dad,

I am not really in the mood to write but wanted to say a few things.

I will never talk to a therapist again about seeing you at the funeral home. I can't forget it, but I won't talk about it.

The two things that I remember the most are how you didn't look like yourself. Your hair wasn't even combed right. And I remember how Grandma sat on the couch in front of your casket. Her tear ducts were definitely working that day. I had never seen her so sad but didn't know how to comfort her.

No one comforted me, either. It felt weird when they tried. I thought Mom would want me to stay close to her side, but she kept going off and talking to people so I spent most of the time alone feeling like I wanted to be anywhere but there.

I was not expecting anyone to be thinking of me, but my best friend Liz and my modern dance instructors, Sue and Janie sent flowers to the funeral home. The funeral home placed the basket with daisies and other spring flowers from Liz on a shelf next to your casket. The ones from my modern dance team and teach-ers were on a table near the couch where Grandma sat the entire time.

I asked Grandma a week or so later if she had seen the flowers from my friends. She said, "Yes, they were beautiful. Especially the purple irises."

It made me feel good that someone noticed that my friends and teachers sent flowers.

love, me

Dear Dad,

It's been a while since I wrote to you. A lot has been happening.

Mom stopped taking me to therapists, but she did make me start talking to Vicar Barber from our church. I still would have liked to talk to Mom instead, but for whatever reason, she won't let me.

Vicar Barber seems to be a nice guy, and he reminded me of you. Is that weird? His first name is Tom, just like yours, and he's silly like you. He is young and has a mustache and sandy brown wavy hair. Mom says he is still in school to be a pastor.

I do like him, but he just talks and talks and talks, Dad!

It is *way* too much. You never talked that much! So, you are very different that way.

I can't always remember what he says because I get distracted. There are always birds chirping outside the stained-glass window and I like listening to them. Anyway, I don't mind visiting with him. After a few visits, I even started telling him more about you.

Sometimes I get sad during my dance performances and get teary thinking about how you used to sit and smile at me from the bleachers. It hurts my heart to not see you there. I also told Vicar that you always liked my crazy costumes.

I tried to hold back my tears, but he said that it was okay to cry. He said crying is healing and helps you work through your emotions. He said that it's not healthy to keep it all inside.

I wasn't sure about his last comment.

Thinking of you used to make me feel good. But lately, it's been the opposite. I feel like it makes me miss you more. Maybe that's why I am not writing you as much?

Vicar always hands me a tissue and tells me to keep sharing.

No one else does this. I wish Mom or Grandma would sit down with a tissue and talk to me.

Anyway, it doesn't matter.

I told Vicar how you liked the itchy poodle skirt I wore for the "Hey Mickey" song by Toni Basil. I told him I would rather have worn my jeans and Indiana Jones T-shirt.

I told him how you said dressing up and being a performer was good for me and helps with feeling nervous.

I also told Vicar about the Halloween that Mom had you dress up like a ballerina. She had you wear a black leotard, tights, and a pink tulle skirt. The funniest part was the ruby red lipstick!

Vicar said that you must have been a really good sport. I told him you were. You were the best.

We have had a lot of nice visits together. In a strange way, I don't feel so alone when I'm visiting him. That makes me feel less upset.

I see him every week and then I ride my bike to Grandma's house and tell her all the stories I told Vicar, like how I would roller-skate around you in the garage while you worked on the riding mower and how we used to sing Kool and Gang's song "Get Down On It" together.

Another one of my favorite times was when you'd finish oiling and gassing up the mower and then we would ride it across town.

I told Vicar how we liked to wave to people when we rode through town and see who would wave back. It felt like we were our very own parade. Vicar also told me that it was very nice of you to cut Aunt Peg's lawn, and Evie's, too! He also told me that you were a good human.

I thought that was such a nice thing to say. It's true, too. I want more people to tell me things about you.

I now mow our lawn every week and my lines look really straight. Every time I finish and see my good work and smell the scent of the cut grass, I think of you and your shiny green John Deere with that big yellow seat.

love, me

Dear Dad,

I don't really want to tell you this, but I am going to.

Something happened a few days ago in school when we were learning about how Native Americans lived off the land. This has been one of my favorite chapters in sixth-grade history. I like how the tribes were resourceful and how they loved and respected nature, like I do.

During this lesson, this boy in my class named Jason—that meanspirited neighbor that has the splotchy face and dirty fingernails—blurted out in front of the entire class, "Why does Shannon look like an Indian?"

I started burning from the inside out. It took everything in me to not get out of my seat and punch him—the way you taught me to punch on Uncle Dane's boxing bag. Or the way, I watched Rocky Balboa try to fight Apollo Creed in, *Rocky*. Which is still my favorite movie of all time.

Instead of punching him, I yelled at him, so everyone could hear me, "I have brown skin from all the hours outdoors with my dad, and at least mine is not gross and grody like yours."

I have never been so mad. I have never wanted to be mean to someone like I was to Jason that day. Mrs. Petro sent him to the principal's office. I wasn't ashamed of my skin, Dad. I was mad at how mean it was for him to make a comment like that.

There are so many times I'd like to say unkind things out loud to lots of people in my life. But I don't! I keep them in because I know it would be wrong.

Life just feels really unfair is all I keep thinking.

Thank goodness for Grandma. She picked me up from school that day and we put a puzzle together. It took my mind off my anger. I was fuming like the fires we made up north.

When I told Grandma what had happened, she said that Jason's parents must not be very nice to him and that I should just ignore him.

I stayed and had dinner with her, which made me feel much better. She made stuffed cabbage and ground beef rolls layered with butter. It was really good.

love, me

Dear Dad,

Vicar Barber left for another church. I miss our talks.

During one of our last visits, I told him about how strange the day of the funeral had felt.

Mom, Shiloh, and I sat in the first pew at the very front of the church and Grandma Rosie sat in the back, in the pew closest to the door. I never understood why. He said that everyone handles death differently. He said that that included me, and that are many stages of grief.

I think this helped me a little. Mom and Grandma are dealing with losing you different from me.

When I got ready to leave, the last thing I said to Vicar Barber was that I didn't know how to stop missing you. When I said that he got up from his creaky wooden chair, came around his desk, and hugged me. I thought that was nice of him but all I could think was that another person I cared for was leaving me.

I wish I knew how to tell Vicar I would miss him. It's not even close to how much I miss you, Dad.

love, me

November 1987–April 1989
Thirteen to Fifteen Years Old

Dear Dad,

It was dark when I woke up today.

I went to the kitchen and made a tuna sandwich on squishy white bread, two handfuls of potato chips, and four baby dill pickles.

Your favorite dinner is what I opted for at breakfast.

There is so much I don't understand, and I don't even know how to begin to try and write it down. My feelings are much bigger than me.

Sometimes, my life feels like the colorful Russian doll I always admire in Great Gram's formal sitting room—that little paper-mâché girl with the colorful headscarf, holding multiple versions of herself, each smaller self perfectly nested inside another identical image of her.

I know it's weird to say that I feel like that doll. But I feel small—like there are many versions of me inside of me, tucked away from all the troubles outside myself.

Vicar Barber once said, "After losing someone we love, we must learn to live without them, but also to live with the love they left behind and within us."

I never really thought about the within part.

You've been gone for almost two years. It is not easy connecting with you when you are no longer with me. Maybe I am confused by what Vicar

Barber said.

I still like to share stories about you and think of you all the time. I try to say silly things to my friends, like your jokes. They don't seem to get them like we did. I also like to play pranks on people. They seem to get these even less.

I loved all your jokes and tricks. I'm going to continue sharing them with everyone. Maybe my friends will eventually get how great they are.

Even though life still seems really hard, writing about our time together is easy even if writing about heart and inside stuff isn't.

love, me

Dear Dad,

Mom and the Dorky Dude are still dating. I overheard her telling one of her ladies at club that they met at a single person gathering. She visits him on the weekends after her last lady, Bertie, leaves. Bertie is still Mom's last lady every Friday.

It's weird to have Mom gone all weekend, every weekend. Even though I am only in seventh grade, Mom doesn't seem concerned about leaving me alone to care for Shiloh. Mom never asks if I'm okay being left in charge. I guess that doesn't surprise me 'cause she doesn't ask how I feel about anything really.

If she did, I'd tell her I feel kind of empty, Dad. You made me feel loved. You spent so much time with me. That is gone now, and it scares me that I'll never have love again. I look for that feeling everywhere, but nothing comes close.

I wish Mom could show me some love. Heck, I wish she was just around more. She's busy working all week so she doesn't really have any time left over for me or Shiloh. And then she leaves us on the weekends.

Mom is still a routine person. Even though I think routine can be boring, it's good to know what to expect. It means I have less to wonder about. I just don't like filling her role and yours for Shiloh and me. I don't think that's bad to say. I don't know any other almost thirteen-year-old that is expected to do what I do.

I do my best, though. I want you to know that. I want to make you proud of me.

love, me

Dear Dad,

Everything has been pretty bad the past few months.

Mom is still never around on the weekends. She seems to really like the Dorky Dude.

I want to talk to my little sister about you, Dad, but I don't know how. She is so innocent. If I am confused, she must be, too. She's only six.

I know Shiloh Anner has to wonder why you left and haven't come back. I remember when she came bouncing into this world seven years after I was born. She was such a sweet baby with her rosy, red cheeks. I would clutch onto her for family pictures or give her a quick kiss on her head before running outside to play.

Everyone at school knows her as my cutesy little sister. A lot of people say we look alike. We both have big brown eyes and a little pug nose.

At four years old, Shiloh was too young to come with us when we would go up north. I always liked having that alone time with you. I guess it was a perk of being older than my sister. I also liked having my alone time with both you and Grandma.

I know Shiloh did not get as much time with you as I did, and now we are learning to live without you *and* Mom, in a way, since she spends too much time hanging out with Dorky Dude.

Now that you aren't here, Shiloh Anner comes with me to Grandma's a lot. She likes laying on the floor with Grandma and drawing in coloring books, too. Pink and orange are her favorite colors. She always signs her name in purple to leave her artistic mark. She still drinks milk from a teal plastic cup with that square handle.

I do like my baby sister. I just don't want to take her everywhere I go. I'm angry at Mom for making me be a parent while she plays house with her new boyfriend thirty miles away. It is so unfair. I do know that I drag Shiloh everywhere, but if I didn't, I would never see my friends.

Dad, she even joined my class when we bobbed for apples, which is my favorite class party game.

Shiloh was mad when I had my seventh-grade talent show and got to dress up and pretend to be Madonna in my lace gloves, layered pearls, poodle skirt, and saddle shoes. I don't think the teachers liked my outfit as much as Shiloh and I did.

Now that I'm in eighth grade, it hasn't gotten any easier. Having your little sister join you on your cheerleading team is not cool. Stuff happens when you are trying to include a little kid in what you do. And more often, I just do not know how to "mother" her.

Maybe I should not tell you any of this, but one-time last year we went to toilet paper an eighth-grade girl's house. Her name is Becky. As we were throwing the paper around, we noticed the local police and we all ran away.

Somehow, Shiloh got left behind. Luckily when I returned to get her, I found that she had hidden behind the big Chestnut tree next to Dr. Gugino's office. She was pretty smart for a little second grader, right?

If Shiloh and I aren't at Grandma's house, then we are basically caring for each other. Well, I take care of her, and she keeps me company.

You would be proud of her dad. She is feisty, like us.

After you died, I started to invent my own explorations. I think this helped me get through the first couple of years of not having you. They definitely helped me take my mind off of Mom dating the Dorky Dude.

My adventures haven't always turned out the way I meant them to, though. Remember when I said earlier that I was looking for love and attention? Well, I want to be truthful, I think I've done a few things for attention, at the expense of Shiloh. I want to tell you about them so I can clear my conscience.

Once, when Shiloh was in second grade, I strapped her into the handmade go-kart my boyfriend, Jacob, had designed. She hit a rock and flipped the cart. Thankfully, she walked away with only a nasty road rash and no broken bones.

I begged her not to tell Mom. I knew I would get in trouble.

I'm not really sure what I was supposed to do. I was in seventh grade and alone with my sister on weekends. I still wanted to have fun.

I also dragged Shiloh to my boyfriend's house so I could make out with him while she watched TV with his little brother. I wore Mom's black lingerie under my T-shirt and jogging pants. I know you wouldn't approve, but nothing bad happened.

That should make you feel a little better.

It felt right at the time.

Mom would be mad if she knew I wasn't being the best sitter with Shiloh. But Mom is the one who keeps leaving her with me. I need my own space. I need to have my friends. I need Mom to be a mom. And I need her to give me some attention.

I don't want to seem selfish or needy, but I don't think what I need is too much to ask for.

The hard thing is, even though I get attention from Jacob, it doesn't seem to make up for the emptiness I feel.

Thinking about all of this makes my head feel really heavy. There are too many thoughts I have spinning around and I can't make sense of what is right and what is wrong.

As I write this, my tears are dripping everywhere.

I keep trying to put all the hurt behind me, but I can't seem to stop the constant flow of memories and anger that flood my mind.

Sorry if this was a lot to read in one letter.

love, me

Dear Dad,

I am back.

I had to walk away and ride my bike around the block a few times after I wrote that last letter.

Confessing isn't easy.

My emotions are too much for me. I have been writing more poems in school. I wrote a few for you and will include them in the folder with all your letters.

There is so much happening right now that it feels over-whelming. I think it's just sometimes easier to think about the past, instead of the pain I now feel.

It makes me feel good to be by myself in my room, talking to you, and thinking about our fun times. It makes the hard parts of the day go away for a while. It's like I can pretend that nothing has changed.

I miss seeing you when I walk to school. I still look for you when I go by Dr. Gugino's office. You would wait for me under the chestnut tree on the opposite side of the street. It's like if I hope hard enough, you might be there waving with a big smile on your face. Even if I could just see you just one more time, I'd be happy.

Remember how I used to fill my rusty red wagon with those spiny looking amoebas? I'd peel them and then throw that smooth brown nut that was inside them into the leaves. Even though raking all of that up was a lot of work, you always let me jump around in the big pile. I was always surprised to hear the pop of those nuts.

I learned from Mr. Grimpo in Science class that chestnuts only explode with sound when they are dry, otherwise they are "duds" and don't make any sound. I bet you already knew that, though.

Even though I still miss you so much that it hurts, I do think I am doing better with school and life, in general.

That should make you feel good.

love, me

Dear Dad,

A few weeks ago, Mom told me we would be moving away from Reese. I am crushed.

I actually feel heartbroken again but for different reasons. I can't even write about it. It makes me too mad. It's been hard enough these last few years getting used to being at school and with my friends and feeling different. Now that I'm in the eighth grade, things have finally gotten a little easier.

And Mom wants to make everything hard again!

How can I leave Grandma? Our house? My friends?

All the memories of you are here in Reese and in this house.

I will no longer have everything around me that feels safe.

Mom and that Dorky Dude are getting married next year. He lives in Hemlock, so we are all moving to his house. It's the same place she's been going every weekend for the past two years. I hate this all so much. I want to vomit.

love, me

The Therapy Sessions
A Note from Tristen, the Therapist

Dear Reader,

It is important to understand that 'doing the work' in therapy is multifaceted. Contributing to your personal development in and outside of therapy sessions is, in my experience, the best way to navigate self-healing. Uncovering your story, layer by layer, is complicated.

Many adults come to therapy when they notice shifting within themselves while navigating their relationship with their partner or their parents. Oftentimes, they need support in a transitional crisis. Most of them want to provide their children with a more evolved version of parenting.

We now know scientifically that the brain and the body have no way to differentiate between physical and emotional trauma. Trauma will reveal itself through physical symptoms like headaches, brain fog, chest pressure, digestive issues, and hypervigilance. Trauma will also reveal itself through emotional symptoms like anxiety, depression, fatigue, aggression, procrastination, insomnia, and coping with stress in unhealthy ways.

Our bodies are already in tune with what our mind and heart still need to process.

Childhood wounding is one of the most complex layers of processing trauma. I highly recommend acquiring a competent therapist you trust and feel safe with to do this intense healing. A healthy therapeutic alliance is essential to unpacking our stories and each of the characters that impacted us for better or worse. In childhood, we develop self-talk, coping mechanisms, and our sense of identity around the experiences we have with the people in our world. Many of us are born into families that don't understand or prioritize emotional intelligence. Many of us inherit generational trauma instead of generational wealth. Many of us had emotionally unsophisticated parents, care givers, teachers, coaches, and extended family members passing on their uninformed, repressed advice.

Emotionally disabled parents are raising emotionally disabled children. These children are repeating the very same unhealthy behaviors, habits, and patterns they've learned from their parents' role modeling and adopted a, "Do as I say, not as I do," mentality. This promotes harmful messaging: *Do what makes me, the adult, comfortable because my needs are more important than your needs as the child.*

We are taught young to orbit other's needs. Families are trapped in generational cycles of ignored, unprocessed emotions. Epigenetics have provided much needed evidence that trauma is passed down repeatedly until someone brave and rebellious enough can break away from the generational pattern.

It's important to remember that all parents parent from their own level of awareness. Most parents are doing the best they can with the skills and tools they had at the time. The concept of exploring childhood wounds is *not* about villainizing parents. I have zero interest in going on fault-finding missions in treatment.

That isn't healthy therapy for anybody. The truth is that your DNA is connected to their DNA, and when we villainize parents, we villainize a genetic part of you.

Most parents love their children and want them to be happy, successful humans. Many parents discover later the themes and patterns that did not help their children to feel emotionally safe. What matters is that we honor it happened. That we begin to develop language around hurt, confusion, and pain in our lives. If you are a parent, I invite you to be more interested in hearing and honoring the pain that your child is willing to share. Even if you feel defensive or remember it differently, tremendous healing is created when we simply say, "Thank you for having the courage to share that. I never realized you saw it that way."

Let's set down any blame and look at trauma with curiosity to uncover dysfunction and replace it with improved mechanisms for coping. We should expand these complicated, messy stories and take the perspectives of each of the contributors of pain. Most importantly, we should learn how to self soothe.

This process allows us to more accurately comprehend that they did the best they could with their level of awareness. This allows us to process childhood wounding to learn healthier ways to mourn our losses, honor and support our inner child, and understand our own story.

I invite you to find a way to process the unresolved grief in your life. Any action, any step is the choice of self-healing. Go to therapy, read the self-help book, walk in nature, cry with a trusted friend, learn to confront your unhealthy patterns, explore something new, talk to your spiritual advisor, listen to the podcast, attend the wellness retreat, journal, ponder, look up at the stars, be playful, go to the class, return to activities and music from your childhood, wander, rest, and always, begin again.

I have no doubt that *you* will heal yourself, just as Shannon has so eloquently and vulnerably shown us she can do.

XOXO
Love, Tristen

Inner Child Session
by Tristen

I open my office door and see a thirty-something mother with beautiful, big eyes and an enormous dose of hesitation. I am used to this.

"Hi Shannon. Welcome! I am thrilled to meet you," I say.

She shakes my hand as she eyes me up and down. I gesture to the couch, and she picks a spot. She immediately pops off with a sarcastic joke. We both laugh and it eases the tension.

"I usually start out with a speech to set the tone for how this works." She nods.

"I am not your typical therapist," I begin. "I am not here to talk about your feelings. We are equals. I believe you have everything within you to heal yourself. I am here to guide you through that process, to point out your blind spots, and to hold you accountable in your journey." Shannon nods, mistrusting.

"I expect we will have to tackle some difficult topics and patterns. In this room, I invite you to talk how you truly talk. Share your truth. I don't give a fuck if you scream, cuss, judge, act vulgar, or cry. I care that you tell the truth and that you grow. We are in this together. I'm not here to carry you—you don't need that."

Her eye twinkles mischievously as she eases back into the cushion.

"If I am doing something that is not a good fit for you, I want you to tell me. Right away. Feedback goes both ways. I want to hear what works for you and what doesn't. It's my job to shift and adjust to your needs, so I need that feedback. Can you agree to that?"

She nods, more agreeable but not relaxed. "Have you been to therapy before?" I ask.

"Many times," she says with a deadpan face. "So where do I start?" "Where it hurts the most," I reply.

She looks around the therapy room. She is either looking to run for an exit or finding some inanimate object to judge me by.

I patiently watch, untroubled by the silence. This one is special. Uncomfortably numb.

I can see the pain prickling behind her smile. I can tell she hasn't had a strong therapist. She's been, many times, but she is a locked vault of secrets. She bravely launches into the details of losing her father. She shares what she is willing to share. She navigates her mourning with a straight face, avoidance, and ambivalence.

I am honored by her trust. I am honored by her share. "Let me start by saying, Shannon, you are whole. You are well. You are powerful. You never gave up against tremendous odds. I want to honor your resiliency." She smiles.

I can tell no one has honored her story in the way she needs.

"Today, we are going to honor the eleven-year-old girl that displayed courage through an impossible loss. A child who did not lose herself or her connection with her father. The girl that would speak her father's name and memory when no one else could. A fighter of truth with no capable adult to guide her."

She stares at me blankly. She says nothing.

I continue. "I want you to put your hands on your heart." She hesitantly complies.

"I want you to close your eyes and, in your mind's eye, picture little Shannon." I pause for a full minute. The clock on the wall is deafening. *Click, click, click.* "Picture if you can that scrappy, skinny, tangled-hair, eleven-year-old. See her smile. See her heart. See her light. Can you see how perfectly imperfect she is?" She nods.

"Now, see her longing for her father. Mourning her strongest, healthiest attachment. An attachment broken for no good reason. See that she has no idea how to handle losing her light-hearted, fun loving, hero." I pause again. She is trying.

"See her, Shannon. See her fear. See her pain. See her confusion."

A single tear lines the left side of her face. She makes no effort to address it.

"You didn't need therapy. You didn't need trouble at school. You didn't need a mother who was so consumed with her own grief that she didn't have the space to manage your grief. You didn't need a demanding little sister. You didn't need your friends to pull away. You didn't need people to pretend it never happened. You didn't need cancer to destroy your family. You didn't your mother distracted by her work and her deepest fear of how she would raise two daughters on her own. You didn't need to learn the world could be so harsh, so young. You didn't need it and you didn't deserve it."

She closes her eyes but allows a faint smile to form.

"You deserve to know that this was *never* your fault. Your feelings were never too much. This was deeply damaging and unfair. This had nothing to do with your value and worth in this world. You can heal yourself; you can honor both of your parents and see they did the best they could with the skills and tools they had at the time. Little Shannon is a superstar, and we honor that she needed truth, comfort, and love in a time of tremendous loss. I want you to comfort eleven-year-old Shannon."

Her eyebrow raises and a distinct pause. Her eyes pop open. The tears are flowing. Unprompted, she closes her eyes again and places her hands back on her heart.

"Can you see little Shannon?" I ask.

"I see her," she whispers.

"What is she doing?"

"She is sitting on the porch. She is alone. She is waiting for a thunderstorm. I can see it swelling in the distance." Another slow smile as she connects with a once familiar scene.

"Go to her," I say. "Go sit next to her on the porch step and tell her who you are."

I wait to allow their conversation to form.

"Tell her that you came today to tell you that it gets better. That you will get through this impossible time. Tell her that one day you will learn to comfort yourself through your grief. That one day your grief will not be this heavy. That you will heal your-self. What do you see?" I ask.

Shannon takes her time. "Little Shannon is smiling! She is leaning into me. She allows me to hug her. She is not afraid. She knows me. She thanks me. She asks me to stay. Can I stay?"

"Yes! You stay as long as she needs you."

I imagine they sit on that porch until that thunderstorm gets closer and it is time for little Shannon to go inside. The tears continue to fall down her face through her smile. We wait. We breathe. Her shoulders soften. Her hands relax. Her closed eyes are still.

"Tell Little Shannon that you are always here for her. You will never abandon her. You will love her unconditionally. You will never forget her." She nods.

"Now thank her, Shannon. Thank Little Shannon for her courage. For her tenacity. For her resiliency. Thank her for honoring her father by speaking his name and remembering his gifts, his good. Thank her for never giving up."

I can see she does.

"Thank her for battling for her life when she felt alone, afraid, discarded. Thank her for trying therapy. For trying church. For journaling and drawing. For eating foods and singing songs that connect her to treasured moments of her father. Thank her for being true to her soul. She is a strong little lady, and she deserves to hear that from you," I add.

She is nodding. And smiling.

We both wait.

"Is it time to go?" I ask.

"Yes," she whispers.

"You can visit Little Shannon any time you like," I state. "She is worthy of any comfort you wish to share. You can connect with her anytime. She will welcome and trust big Shannon forever forward."

Ever so slowly she opens her eyes. She inhales and moves her hands from her heart to reach the three-ply tissue box. She rapidly pulls out tissues—one, two, three, four!

A long, slow exhale follows.

The Mother Wound Session
by Tristen

Today is a disaster. I am running behind schedule, back logged on emails and texts, and I haven't had time to eat my lunch in between back-to-back sessions.

Shannon walks in with similar energy. She has some notes and scattered thoughts that center around the challenges of parenting. "I cannot handle this never-ending conflict between the boys. I know this is an age and stage thing, but it is impossible to navigate. I'm exhausted. I feel like a referee all day long."

"Let's explore how you would like your home to feel, Shannon. Take a moment to settle in and center yourself. Take a big cleansing breath, close your eyes, and notice how you want your home to feel. I want you to describe in detail exactly how you wish it would *feel* in your home. Notice the environment. Notice the level of tension. Notice the interactions between you, Tim, and the boys. Notice the way you solve problems and navigate conflict. What do you see?"

"I envision an environment with low tension. A place where it is safe to let your guard down. A place where we all feel secure, connected. A space that is clean, full of laughter, and engaging conversation. I want my home to feel calm. I want Tim and I to be loving and attentive to one another and our boys. I want their friends to come over and feel relaxed. I want it to be a comfortable place for anyone who enters. I want Cole and Cody to share their thoughts, express their feelings, and value vulnerability." We both can feel this secure space she's describing.

A healthy family system.

"I want it to be everything I didn't have growing up," she adds.

"There it is, Shannon. Your childhood need surfaces," I say. "It is natural for our unmet childhood needs to be what we most desire to give our own children. You are likely putting pressure on yourself to be a perfect parent, fostering a magical home life, and childhood for your boys.

This most likely is connected to your own process of reparenting." "Reparenting?" she repeats.

"Reparenting means learning a skill that wasn't regularly modeled or taught to you in your childhood environments. Oftentimes, we don't even realize *it* was missing until we notice *it* existing in a friend's home where we feel safe or discover *it* when parenting our own children one day. In an ideal family system, our parents are two stable, conscious, self-actualized people who allow their children to be seen and heard as the unique individuals that they are. This sophisticated parenting method means allowing children to be who they are, not who we think they should be. The truth is that we live in a world that does not prioritize emotional intelligence or self-awareness as a top tier parenting skill. Most of us were raised by emotionally disabled parents. Parents who were detached, emotionally neglectful, uncomfortable with tears and big emotions, unconscious, avoidant people," I state.

"If they provided a roof over our head, food on the table and access to education, they truly believed they did their job. Little Shannon was craving connection and thirsty for deep engagement. She was longing for a calm, predictable home environment that promoted healthy autonomy and the ability to have difficult conversations. She was looking for comfort, laughter, a safe space. Well, guess what! Big Shannon is running this shit now, and she can create exactly what she needed and exactly what her boys need now," I say with enthusiasm.

She smiles as she resonates with her own healing power.

"I believe our healing truly begins when we discover the opportunity to mother ourselves and tend to our inner child. This becomes even more profound when we reparent ourselves as we simultaneously parent our own children. Each of these are personal responsibilities. Let's talk about this process of motherhood and how it intersects with not only reparenting yourself, but also the parallels of what it brings up regarding your mom as a mother."

"Well, buckle in because that is a complicated relationship!"

"As all mothers are," I confirm with a smile.

Shannon details dysfunctional dynamics with her mom throughout childhood and adolescence, layered with profound themes of emotional pain, deep loneliness, poor boundaries, parentification, and helplessness.

"There are so many survival tactics weaved into your conditioning," I say, "creating an unclear sense of self and high tolerance for being treated poorly. You learned to make your needs small to accommodate your mom's needs while desperately longing for your mom to offer guidance and acceptance. This is the Mother Wound," I honor. "Navigating the Mother Wound means deep diving into the cultural traumas and intergenerational complexities of not only your worth but those same needs for your mother, her mother, and all the mothers before her. Processing through attachment wounding and emotional neglect is at its core—analyzation of the breakdown of trust. Your unresolved emotions embedded limiting beliefs creating consequential loss of trust.

This had a profound impact on your self-esteem, your ability to feel safe and seen in the world, as well as who you gravitated to as a life partner.

"Your parentified role in your family growing up became the blueprint for all your relationships. Interpersonal relationships that mimic complicated and strained interactions, like with your mom, feel familiar. Your childhood survival tactics feel natural, emotionally supporting others your harmful default. You became accustomed to avoiding conflict to keep the peace, shrinking yourself to fit in, people pleasing tendencies, accommodating the emotionally immature. You became incredibly sophisticated at emotional care taking. Tragically, to the point of self-abandonment and resentment.

"The Mother Wound commonly shows up in our relationship with our partner. When we are starved emotionally, all we really want is a partner that can provide the emotional warmth we craved in childhood. Unfortunately, we often attempt to heal this wound by seeking partners that are emotionally repressed and hard to reach. Our partner becomes who we emotionally sponsor as unresolved cycles linger in the background of our mistrusting thoughts and relationship choices."

I can see her digesting quickly, in real time. She is a perceptive learner. "Am I seeking to heal the Mother Wound in my relationship with Tim?" she asks.

"I think you can answer that better than I can," I respond. "If you notice a pattern of polarized needs in your marriage—a deep desire to be cared for and an equally difficult ability to trust—then we have more work to do. If you feel toxic shame and emotionally unsupported in your marriage, then we have more work to do. If you notice a pattern where you do the bulk of the heavy emotionally lifting, then we definitely have more work to do.

"Perhaps what is triggering in your relationship with Tim is when you sense parallels to your mom's disengagement. Your trauma is informing you that you feel disappointed. While your mom was consumed with her single parenting and lack of language to describe the impact of domestic violence from her deceased husband and second husband, you grappled with feeling invisible and deeply craved security. It was never your responsibility to make up for your mom," I insist. "And it is not your responsibility to do this in any of your relationships. Trust me when I tell you that your mom's behaviors have everything to do with her and very little to do with you. Her pain was subconsciously projected onto you, fragmenting your sense of self. Letting go of these internalized patterns helps to break the generational trauma as well as set free your own fears about what kind of mother you hope to be."

She relaxes. It clicks. She smiles.

"Your mission is to explore, outside of this therapy room, what might be happening within yourself when you notice yourself slipping into limiting beliefs and codependency of managing the mood for any person or environment. Look for more complicated feelings connected to the Mother Wound. Do you feel disappointed? Invisible? Dismissed? Unimportant? Devalued? Alone? I want you to truly sit with the feeling and find an accurate label. Like a little label maker. And once you find it, ask yourself, 'How is this feeling familiar? What is this emotional flooding trying to teach me about myself? What are other times in my life that feel similar to this moment, to this feeling? How can I best comfort and take care of myself now that I understand this more fully?'"

"Shannon," I continue, "your home is full of love. Your boys feel secure and safe. You put tremendous pressure on yourself to meet their needs.

You are emotionally available and allow them to be who they are. This includes when they are battling for parental attention or over video games or who gets the front seat. Think of the many ways you show up for them, champion them, and promote their individuality. You are a great mom! You are the best mom they could ever ask for! You are healing little Shannon every time you reparent yourself and parent them from a place of emotional intelligence."

We both smile, knowing this is true. She really is a great mom.

"I want you to conceptualize reparenting the Mother Wound as an important, lifelong tool," I declare. "*Gift*, not give, yourself what you desperately needed as a child. This is how we can begin to heal. This is how we create a marriage that *feels* safe. This is the best way to pull your unmet childhood needs out of hiding and into the light."

She smiles knowingly as the healing shifts back within her control.

PART II

The Angry Years

Dear Reader,

Someone once asked me, "Who hurt you?"

I replied, "My own expectations."

At eleven years of age, one does not expect or even fathom losing a beloved parent. To be robbed of that one seemingly simple expectation was jolting.

Now, with a lens that spans fifty years—encompassing years of experiences, lessons, and growth—I fully realize that the ebbs and flows of life, and the many challenges I faced defined my character and shaped my destiny. My journey through life has been such a mosaic of moments— difficult, delightful, and everything in between—to shape the person that I am today.

As I navigated the turbulent waters of grief as a young girl, coupled with moving away from my safe space, I simultaneously confronted the dynamics of living with a manipulative stepfather and an emotionally uninvolved mother.

These relationships tested my resilience and taught me profound lessons about strength, self-worth, and the true meaning of family.

I came to understand how difficult it is to navigate relationships with self-absorbed figures, particularly when they hold positions of authority or influence.

My first lesson in narcissistic behavior came early on—a battle for self worth when my stepfather entered the picture, shortly after my father's death. While I might have hoped this man would provide some semblance of paternal guidance, I found that his constant need for control and validation overshadowed any possibility of genuine concern or empathy. By default, he was prone to dominate and put others down. And, while I felt strong enough to ignore it, his jabs still affected me.

I watched his behavior erode my mother's self-esteem, making it difficult for her not only to protect herself, but also my little sister. Though I was only fourteen, I felt the need to always be on high alert. His emotional volatility created an unstable home environment. His outbursts were unpredictable and further provoked if I did not follow his rules and actions. Everyone walked on eggshells, attempting to avoid triggering his anger. He never scared me, which was the odd part.

Protecting my mom and sister was a heavy responsibility. During those formative years, the burden of knowing that my mom chose this toxic and domineering man over the well-being of her children weighed heavy on my heart. And the need to constantly intervene—to try to shield both my mother and sister from this man's wrath—was emotionally draining. It left me feeling isolated and alone, as I had no one to turn to for support or understanding other than my boyfriend's family at the time.

As I grew older, my desire for independence increasingly clashed with my stepfather's rage and need for control. Not until things finally boiled to a point where my mother could see the dangerous trajectory that was unfolding did she finally accept help to move out and leave this man when I was eighteen years old.

During these years, I learned to navigate the trenches by developing bad habits that would take me years to understand and unlearn.

Like many of you, people pleasing and self-sacrificing became a way of life, something that nearly did me in but ultimately, I realized, was something else I could overcome.

love, me

December 1987 to April 1989
Thirteen to Fifteen Years Old

Dear Dad,

I don't think it's okay to feel as furious as I do at thirteen years old. Mom is making us move. I'm always watching my younger sister. I feel like I'm not allowed to find my own way and now everything I've ever known is going to be ripped away from me.

When I think about what the next few years will be like, I get so angry that I just want to throw things, or punch things.

I need this anger to go somewhere.

Maybe everything is finally catching up to me. Maybe watching Shiloh has been too much and I'm finally feeling that pressure. Or maybe this is just what being almost fourteen feels like without a dad. Or an indifferent mom who is not mothering me if I'm really being honest.

Being around my friends and seeing them with their families feels more and more complicated. I was having dinner at Liz's a few nights ago and her whole family was sitting around the table. I don't have a "whole" family anymore, and Shiloh, Mom, and I definitely don't sit around the table together.

Not one of my friends has had a parent die.

The one thing I could count on to make me feel safe was our home. I can still feel my dad there and remember our times together. Now it is being taken away, too.

love, me

Dear Dad,

What Mom is doing is just mean. Everything I feel is fuzzy. My thoughts are crushing my insides and hurt my heart. I do not want to move away from the town I've grown up in. The thought of leaving Grandma sickens me. She is my rock. I will miss seeing the pile of raked leaves each Fall and the pop of the nuts. I'll miss riding my bike to the Dairy Barn and eating drippy chocolate-dipped cones. I'll miss climbing the tree behind the garage. I'll miss Irene's lilac shrub and sticking my head into the purple flowers. They smell like perfume.

I will miss the uneven sidewalks and hanging on to Grandma's car while riding my skateboard so I can bounce over the crack in the street. Every time she catches me, she tells me to let go so I don't get hurt. I wonder if anyone else ever noticed that flaw in the street.

I wonder if people see my scars. Not just the ones on my knees from running and riding my bike too fast. I miss everything here, but most of all my memories with Dad were made here.

I wrote this poem last week. Mr. Grimpo gave me a gold star sticker in the top left corner of my paper and said, "Keep it up. Great work" when he handed it back to me.

My Broken Heart
My tears fall like rain
I still feel the pain
Broken heart and shattered dreams
Nothing quite as it seems
Mom's hug is not the same
Dad's love lost in the rain
I wish I could be a bird
Fly away from the hurt and never be heard
My wounded wings
I may never again know how to sing
Within my heart—sad and blue
There is no more love to see me through
SH

I hope this doesn't make you sad, too, Dad.

love, me

Dear Dad,

It has been a long time since I wrote to you. I am trying to be in a better mood, but it is hard.

I don't think I would get out of bed if I didn't have to. Everything hurts, especially my head and my heart. Even my neck has pain in it, like yours did before you got cancer.

I think about cancer. I think about dying.

I don't know how to make sense of my feelings, but I do see and feel darkness, but I am not afraid of it. I am crumbling, but I am fighting through my fear like you taught me to do, and I know it's my job to protect myself and Shiloh since Mom won't.

I don't have money to live on my own with Shiloh. If I did, I would.

I have proven that I can take care of us. If I can stay at home alone with Shiloh every weekend, cut the lawn, make dinner, and do the list of chores Mom makes before she leaves, I can do anything.

I feel better when I write to you.

It's like writing about our memories and what's going on here gives me the energy I need to keep going.

Mom sold your John Deere. Actually, she got rid of all your things. All I have of you are our adventures. They are all safely stashed in my mind. I guess that's really better than having your old shirts or hats anyway.

In English today, Mr. Grimpo said, "Storytelling offers a sense of safety by creating spaces for exploration and expression." I liked that.

Writing to you helps me let go of all the emotions trapped inside me but want to break free. Storytelling with you, gives me a feeling of safety when everything else feels so unsafe right now.

The other day, Grandma started calling Mr. Grimpo "Mr. Grumpy." I giggle every time she does it.

Mr. Grimpo was our principal, but now he's teaching most of my classes. I think Grandma calls him grumpy because he always has a frown on his face. Grandma can be pretty clever when she wants to be.

I like the way Mr. Grimpo teaches English. He pushes me to be more descriptive in my writing in order to give readers reference points. I enjoy writing and learning how to be a better storyteller.

Writing to you is great practice in getting better at storytelling. I'm going to start trying to use the stuff I learn in English when I write to you. I hope you like my tales. I have many to share.

Some of my tales may not be appropriate to share with you. I am still deciding if I should.

It can't hurt, is what I tell myself. So, I'm going to start sharing more with you, Dad. These stories overpower me, and I need to get rid of them.

I may feel lighter after.

Here we go…

First, I should tell you a smidgen of the "backstory," as Mr. Grimpo calls it. He told us that the backstory in a written piece gives context to a reader. It's another way of describing the setting and why things occur. He reminded me of that in red ink on one of my papers.

So, here's some of the backstory…

A few years ago, Mom started dating this very tall man from Hemlock—a town located an hour away from Reese. For anyone who has never been there, my guess is that it sucks. .

It seemed like it got pretty serious pretty quick. This guy has a small head and hardly any hair. He's nothing special. He's just a small-headed, no-hair man who built the house that he lives in.

His house is surrounded by woods and ditches with tall cattails. His neighbors are not close by, but close enough to run to or borrow something. Mom says she started dating him at the beginning of 1986, but I think it was the end of 1985 and you had only been gone a few months. I am not sure any of our relatives would believe that Mom would leave me and Shiloh every weekend to flit off to see a new boy toy so soon after you died. But she did. This makes me mad.

Sorry, Dad, that might seem disrespectful but it's how I feel. I despise Mom right now, and if you could help me to not feel that way, even just a little, it would be a gift. I will try to be more respectful as I continue. I know this is what you always taught me to be.

Mom made me visit the dorky guy's house twice. (I'm not being disrespectful, it's just kind of who he is).

Not only does he have a tiny, bald head, but he also has a nose that is pointy and long. It's not even close to cute, like Shiloh's button nose. So, he does look kind of dorky.

Anyway, his house truly is in the middle of nowhere. I can't walk to a Speedy Q for cheesy nachos with ground beef or ride my bike anywhere.

I keep forgetting to tell you that Mom bought me a blue ten-speed. I think you would like it. Mom won't let me cruise the streets because there aren't any sidewalks. If we need a carton of milk, we have to get in a car and drive at least fifteen minutes to the nearest store.

I feel totally N-U-M-B to everything that is around me.

I am just going through the motions. Life sucks big time right now, and there is nothing I can do about it.

I do my best to function without wanting to tell everyone around me that they are pricks. (You used that word and told me not to repeat it, but I like the way it sounds when I say it.) Anyway, the people around me are supposed to protect me, right? Not the other way around! I'm tired of being the adult. It just seems wrong.

But hey, what do I know? I am only a measly eighth grader who is being forced to leave the only home I've ever known, the only place that I feel safe in, and I'm expected to have no feelings or say in the matter.

love, me

Dear Dad,

I need to vent. (Sorry if it seems like that's all I do lately.) I am devastated and have no idea what to do about it. Mom's routine absence has finally set me off! She continues to be gone almost *every* weekend and just leaves Shiloh with me. I have become overly responsible for my little sister, and I just know that this isn't right.

I am in eighth grade and want to hang out with my friends and not have to take my baby sister with me everywhere I go. I don't think that's unfair to ask of Mom. I get that I might need to help out here and there, but it's gotten completely out of hand.

I started watching Shiloh before I even turned twelve. Who leaves an eleven-year-old and four-year-old home alone for days?

Being left alone to care for my four-and-a-half-year-old sister is not something I want to do on a permanent basis.

I would rather be on the basketball court or in gym class climbing the rope. I want to be free, like my friends.

I miss being a kid.

And I miss someone making dinner for Shiloh and me.

I never wonder what Mom is doing when she leaves us every weekend. I've gotten used to not missing her. But I do wish she would leave us one of those casseroles that she'd always make for our family functions. Or maybe just some money, so I could buy nachos or candy at Speedy Q. I still eat the head off those chubby, spicy, cinnamon gummy bear candies first.

Since Mom is the queen of the hot dish, you'd think she would think to leave us with some food.

The one good thing is Shiloh has always been easy to make stuff for. She never really complains too much, except maybe when I make her eat Cream of Mushroom soup. This has been one of my specialty dinners.

It kind of reminds me of Grandma's gravy, only whiter and with rubbery mushrooms.

I will say that it's super easy to just heat up, which makes getting dinner easy, but Shiloh hates it. Sometimes, after seeing her face, I make her eat it just to be mean. I know that sounds terrible, but I think I just get frustrated with what I'm expected to do.

I figure if I can eat that soup and survive, then she will, too.

I have to admit, though, that after a lot of weekends of eating mushroom soup that Shilo his probably right. After a few dinners, it's not so great. I think it belongs best in casseroles, not on its own.

Sometimes I'll also make Spaghetti O's with beef franks. Shiloh likes the meatball version better, but I think they are kind of gross because they always look like they have white, knobby pieces in them, which I don't think should be there.

I think I learned to be a good eater and not complain early on. I remember being told that children are to be seen and not heard and that we are supposed to eat everything on our plate because there are starving children in Africa.

I never really understood the intimidation of those two things, but I always obeyed. I tried to get Shiloh to also obey those rules, but she just complains, takes two bites, and leaves the rest for me.

Anyway, I don't have the energy to try to enforce those rules that I was always reminded of, so I don't.

Sometimes, I try to get fancy. I'll take chicken noodle soup and mix it with white rice and then serve it in Mom's nice black stone bowls. They are the ones she only uses for her club ladies. I figure she's not around and doesn't bother to leave us anything to eat, so I just do it and don't tell her.

To make it extra special, we'll eat our soup sitting cross-legged together on the living room floor. I turn our laundry basket upside-down to use as our table and we pretend we are having a "cultural" dining experience. It's kind of cool to pretend like we are doing something that people in India, China, or Japan are doing, even if our food is canned soup.

A lot of nights, after we finish eating, we'll play with our Barbie dolls. I like to use flashlights to pretend like our Barbies are performing on a stage. One night, our neighbor called us because she saw all the flashing of light and was concerned an intruder was in the house. I told her we were okay and just having fun.

When Mom got home, I told her what had happened because I figured she'd find out from Terry's mom. We didn't get in any trouble, but I do wonder what Terry's mom thinks of Mom leaving us alone. The good thing is Shiloh acts more and more like my little partner in crime. She just plays along.

I guess what Mr. Grimpo said to me a few days ago is true... "Creativity is something, Shannon, you are not short on." I think he was giving me a compliment. I'll take it.

love, me

Dear Dad,

Today, I am writing in red ink. It matches the color of my heart.

I decided to take my bike and visit your grave on the outskirts of town.

The big, tall pine that towers over where you are buried is still there. It's a nice setting but sap falls all over your headstone. That sticky stuff just oozes from that tree. I always bring a towel with paint remover, but it doesn't help much.

I sat on the soft grass and talked to you. I wonder if you can hear me. I hope so.

There are only two more weeks before Mom is making us move away from Reese. I can't believe it's even happening, but she's been dating this guy for three years, so I guess she figures she has to make it official, even if it feels wrong to me.

I am graduating from eighth grade and had my confirmation party at the Richville American Legion hall, but the party felt flat. I liked my dress. Knowing my friends and I will be separated sucks. I want to be a Reese Rocket not a Valley Lutheran Charger.

They are getting married in June. It just makes me so angry. I can't even describe it. To be honest, there are so many things I am angry about ... way too many to list. Maybe I can tell you more later.

Mainly, I am just sick and tired of feeling this non-stop, roller coaster of feelings. The ups and downs I feel just seem like too much to take. Don't get me wrong, I like a good roller coaster. Remember those steep slopes and open carriages on the coaster we rode at Cedar Point?

It would go so fast.

It makes me a little teary eyed to think of how much we loved the thrill of all those rides and those soft pretzels with the goopy nacho cheese.

The roller coaster I feel like I'm riding now, Dad, is nothing like Cedar Point! Aat least a real roller coaster will eventually stop and let you off. And you can choose not to ride it.

I have *no* choice now. I'm being forced to take a ride I don't want to take, and it makes me feel sick. Life seems like an endless road of twists and turns, and I'm just being pushed along without any say.

I wish Mom would slow down her decisions. If she did, she might do something else, maybe stay in Reese and be a real mom to me and Shiloh. I think if she did, this roller coaster of emotions I feel would stop.

What do I do? I feel stuck. There's so much anger building inside of me that I might explode. I want to fight back and stop Mom from marrying the Dorky Dude. I want to stay in Reese with my friends, my school, and Grandma. And every time I think of this, it makes me sad because fighting back wouldn't do anything, no one would listen.

I am learning life doesn't care.

Those who should love and protect me don't.

So, I smile and pretend I'm okay. Inside, I hope that the awful ride I'm on ends soon and I can jump off.

love, me

Dear Dad,

Memories of you calm me.

Today I'm writing to you in green ink, using one of my favorite pens— a Bic, four-color retractable pen. Whoever designed this was clever. I love that you can switch between colors with a simple click. If my mood changes, I can just pick a different color. I like matching colors of ink to my mood when I'm writing. Sometimes, I use all the colors on one page.

When I think about my early childhood memories, being at your mom's and dad's farmhouse in Richville might be my favorite.

I smile every time I think of our visits with Grandpa and Grandma. Their house was terrific. I liked how it felt like it was in the middle of nowhere even though it was only five minutes away from Reese. Maybe because it was in the woods.

It wasn't a fancy place, but it was cozy. It stood tall and proud and had that wrap-around porch with the creaky stairs. There were all those red barns in the back where Keenan, their border collie, would sleep. I used to keep my green plastic bat and white whiffle ball in the smallest barn along with the garden tools and Grandpa's grill.

Those were some fun times, even though I hardly ever talked to Grandpa. I'd just kind of run past him without really saying much. I can still see him standing at the kitchen counter smoking his cigarette and drinking a beer out of a short glass. He always wore those black, thick rimmed glasses. I thought it was funny that his glasses matched his jet-black hair.

Who would have thought someone could love an old, distressed, shingled-sided farmhouse with chipping paint set out in the middle of farm country so much! Mr. Grimpo would be proud of that sentence. He would say that I was being very illustrative in my writing.

Are you noticing the difference in my style?

How cool it must have been to grow up there with Grandma Rosie.

Even though she doesn't live at that farmhouse anymore, she still works as a waitress at Fritz's. Remember when we visited her there and I had frog legs for the first time?

I'm glad Grandma Rosie stayed working at Fritz's. It's nice to have some things stay the same in life. I always thought she looked cute in her uniform with the lacy apron.

Even though Fritz's is a little dark and dingy, the food is okay and it's fun meeting all of Grandma's friends. I think the salad bar buffet is probably the best thing to order; except I could never correctly use the red plastic tongs to grab the croutons. I guess other people had trouble with those tongs, too, because I always found black olives in the shredded cheddar. That bothered me.

Of all of Grandma's friends, I think I liked her friend Dorothy the best. She always made me a Shirley Temple and put three cherries in it along with a plastic monkey. It's funny how Grandma had two friends named Dorothy. And both of them are nice.

I don't think I ever told you this, but I am glad it was Grandma Rosie, and not Mom's mom, who looked after me from when I was little. Even though I would have liked to be with you and Mom, going to the farmhouse was special. There was a lot to explore with all those barns and all that land. I got lost within myself and the world around me.

Sometimes, when I was at the farmhouse, Grandma would take me to that gas station with the general store attached. Every time I went there, I'd get a scoop of Blue Moon. That was the brightest blue ice cream I had ever seen, and it tasted just like the sweetest sugar cereal. I would take my time enjoying it, hoping it wouldn't melt too quick. And even though I wanted it to last forever, I'd still give the last two bites of the cone to Keenan. There wasn't much ice cream left in those two bites, but Keenan liked the cone better anyway.

On nice days, Grandma and I would have a picnic underneath one of the trees that dotted their property. I liked sitting cross-legged next to her eating our lunches or snacking on burnt peanuts.

On Tuesday afternoons, I'd sit with the neighbor girl on the bed of her family's large tractor-trailer, helping sell the vegetables her family grew on their farm. There were always these mouthwatering, juicy, ripe red tomatoes, ears of yellow corn (sometimes with worms running through the bins they were in), and oversized cucumbers that looked fake.

Sarah was the little girl's name. I thought she was really nice, and I liked selling stuff. One time I tried to sell some stalks of rhubarb that I had picked from Grandma's garden without anyone knowing. I figured if I made the sale on my own, then I deserved to keep the money.

I eventually had to confess what I had done when Grandma Rosie found the money that I had made in one of my pockets and asked where it came from. I didn't lie. You taught me that.

Grandma and I would also play baseball out in front of the farmhouse. Thinking back, I bet there weren't a lot of grandmas who did that. Mine was special. She always seemed up for some fun.

I long for those feelings again. You wouldn't believe how many times I've thought of those times with Keenan since you died. I feel so overwhelmed by everything right now that just thinking of that safe place with Keenan helps me calm down.

It just seems so sad, Dad, that all those times are now just memories for me. I like having them to think about, but I wish I was living those times and not just remembering them.

I sometimes think that my memory-making times are over.

Sorry for always writing to you about how sad I feel. I know it was probably fun for you to remember the farmhouse and

Grandpa and Grandma. And not so fun to know that I'm not feeling so great about life right now.

love, me

Dear Dad,

I visited the cemetery today. As I sat there by your grave, all these memories of our favorite times together flashed through my head.

I really don't know what to think. I'm happy that we had such good times together and I get lost in those thoughts. And then, I look around and it hits me that I'm in a cemetery. A cemetery!

This is all so wrong. I don't think I'll ever be okay. I'm not sure how long I was there. I think I just started daydreaming and I lost track of time. I was thinking how great it would be if you were still alive and breathing.

I do think, though, that you'd be pleased to know that it's super quiet and peaceful there.

The people who come, visiting whoever it is they visit, don't make a lot of sounds. Well … unless they are my mom!

I was sitting there today just thinking about how peaceful it seemed when I suddenly heard Mom shouting at me from the car. I sprang up and looked back, a little embarrassed at how loud she had shouted. She was obviously in a rush to get home because she had the car door wide open and was waving for me to get in, like we were late for something.

It annoyed me! I hurried back to the car, her new gray Grand Am. I missed the red Cutlass. Mom asked me if everything was okay. I have waited so long for her to ask that I didn't know how to answer. I'm obviously *not* "okay" if I'm visiting my dad at a cemetery. It seemed like such a dumb question.

I wish Mom would say, "I miss your dad, too." I want her to hug me. I want her to say that we do not have to move. I can't talk to her. The whole situation infuriates me.

I wish I could tell her how trapped I feel. That my insides feel like they are in knots. That I feel completely alone even when she's with me.

I want her to tell me she is *done* with the Dorky Dude.

I'm learning, though, that it doesn't matter what I say or how I silently suffer. We will still move.

I ended up telling Mom that I was okay. It is just easier.

I have so many mixed feelings about starting a new high school, meeting new friends, and leaving everything I know and love behind.

Mom went straight to the kitchen to make dinner when we got home, so I went outside where you and I spent so much time together. I can still feel you there. I can see you chipping golf balls out on the lawn. It's weird to think I won't be able to walk outside and have these memories once we move away.

I also walked over to Eric's house to see if he was home and might want to play some basketball. We get together almost every day after school to play H-O-R-S-E. We both get pretty competitive and play about the same, but I haven't been able to duplicate the three-point hipshot he can sometimes make.

Since Eric wasn't home and it started raining, I decided to walk over to the Video Venture down the street. Before I got a few houses down, I could hear Mom yelling my name. At first, I ignored her because she'd told me I had an hour to kill before dinner and it hadn't been that long. Then I heard her yell for me again and I saw she was in the street, waving for me to come home. I thought this was odd, so I went back.

You won't believe this, Dad. I got called home to see Dorky Dude standing in our house!

This was obviously why Mom was so antsy at the cemetery, so in a rush to get home and get dinner started.

I was so shocked to see this guy in our house, standing in front of the fireplace where you and I used to wrestle, smiling with these abnormally straight, white teeth. It's like his whole smile seems fake and way, way too big. His teeth are too perfect. Nobody has teeth that are that straight and clean. Not even Dr. Zaleski, our dentist.

And Dorky Dude has these piercing brown eyes that don't seem kind. His eyes and fake smile make me not trust him. There's something off about him and his energy, but Mom always seems happy around him, so I try to be polite.

He started to talk to me about basketball, but I could not stop looking at his teeth.

I wanted to run, see if Eric had gotten home, anything but be with Dorky Dude. Mom told him to have a seat while she checked on dinner, leaving me standing there. He sat down on our brown plaid couch, and I snickered inside thinking of when we ate that vanilla ice cream with Hershey chocolate syrup drizzled on top and I spilled some. You rubbed it in and said that the chocolate would blend in with the color of the couch.

We never told Mom and she never saw the stain, but I thought it was funny that Dorky Dude sat on it and didn't even know.

He started to talk to me about basketball again. All I could think of was that I would soon be living in the same house with this tall, Dorky Dude with straight, white teeth.

What if he wanted to play basketball with me?

What if he wanted me to call him Dad?

What if he tries to discipline me for talking back to Mom?

I decided I would be polite, like I was taught, and use my manners. For you, for Mom, and for myself and Shiloh. I don't want to be labeled the troublemaker. Too often lately, people say I am sassy or not following the rules when I push back. But I know in my heart of hearts that they are wrong. I understand more than they think I do about what is happening.

Having dinner with Mom's boyfriend, I realized I can sink, or I can swim. I am going to try to swim. It's tiring, but I know I can do it.

I mean, I am for real, a pretty good swimmer. I loved learning to swim because you were a good swimmer. And when I finally got good enough, you and I would go swimming in Lake Ontario at Drummond Island. Jumping off the dock was one of my favorite things to do.

I will N-E-V-E-R forget when we were getting out of the water one time when I was maybe four. I freaked out because I saw a rattlesnake coming toward me.

"Don't flee dangerous situations like these, Shannon. Do the opposite," you said.

You killed the snake with a shovel.

You talked to me about having an instinct to avoid injury, that sometimes it's better to be calm and still. You called it "self-preservation."

I am not sure if this is the same thing, Dad, but I knew I couldn't run away from having dinner with Mom's boyfriend. I knew I had to face my fear head-on.

So, I continued talking with the smiley, straight-toothed man and pretended he was someone I wanted to be around to make Mom happy.

The good thing is that he rarely comes around. Mom spends most of her time with him alone at his house in Hemlock. I'm thinking my reaction tonight has something to do with what happened once when he *did* stay at our house in Reese. It was a really dark moment. It was at the end of my seventh-grade year.

I feel bad telling you this now, but I want to get it off my chest. Maybe I won't think about it anymore then. I hate it when it comes back to me. Every time it does, I wish I had just run to Jacob's house that night and never returned, but I stayed against my better judgment.

I should have pounded on the wall. It makes me sick thinking about it.

I think it's best to just say it... I heard loud moaning sounds coming from yours and Mom's bedroom one night when the Dorky Dude stayed overnight. The sounds I heard actually woke me up.

I was unsure of what I should do, and I didn't want to even think about what the sounds meant.

I don't know why, but I got up and tiptoed past the living room, into the hallway, and stood by the bathroom near *your* room.

I was mortified by the sounds I heard and wanted to pound on the bedroom door, to stop what was going on. But I didn't. To this day, I am mad at myself for not doing that, but I think in that moment I just froze.

I only hoped that Shiloh was sound asleep.

I felt ashamed and afraid. My body was nervous and contorting in a way I could not explain. Those sounds and the image of what was going on behind that bedroom door will forever be etched in my heart and head.

Overhearing Mom and the shitty, smiling man have sex together was both dirty and disgusting. All I could do was suppress the bubbling blood flow in my brain and return to bed.

My life felt doomed. I felt like that moment marked the beginning of the end. That room and that bed was where I'd always go when summer storms raged. I'd lay my head on your chest, hearing the soothing rhythm of your heartbeat, until I finally fell asleep.

Hearing what Mom and the Dorky Dude did together in that room left me scarred.

I wanted to tell someone, but who? Feelings just keep piling up inside me. Sharing some of this with you helps me feel like I'm not drowning.

I also know you and I can handle tough stuff, but this is exhausting and never seems to end.

love, me

Dear Dad,

Today, I am writing to you in black ink only.

Everything feels like it is happening too fast. I feel like I keep drowning in my sea of thoughts. Mom somehow must know I heard her and the Dorky Dude that night and maybe sensed a change in me because she brought up that therapist with the scurvy fish tank again.

She asked me, out of the blue, if I might want to speak to him. I wonder if she feels badly about her behavior because she asked me in a way that was both kind and weird. As usual, though, she doesn't try to talk to me herself, or explain anything, she just tries to pawn me off on someone else ... always a stranger.

She never gets it that the only person I long to talk to is her. She's the only parent I have left here.

I turn to you, because there's no one here I can talk to.

It would be really hard now to try and verbalize what I am experiencing because I've had to stuff my emotions and experiences so deep inside me, for so long now, that I don't know how to reach them.

I want to be my own person. I want to be strong. I want to be happy.

The problem is that there is so much to handle on my own—responsibilities and feelings—that it feels like too much. I'm pulling away from who I am.

Life keeps taking me further and further away from you, Dad.

Watching the decisions that Mom is making makes me resent her.

I am hurt by how Mom is behaving, and I feel misunderstood. It's a whole new kind of pain, different than your death. Thanks for listening.

love, me

Dear Dad,

No kid who loves their dad wants another dad to try to replace him.

I want to say that because I don't want you to think that I'm making stuff up just because I don't want Mom to bring another man into our lives. I don't. But that's not the reason I don't like the Dorky Dude.

If you were my therapist, like the guy with the scurvy fish tank, I would tell you when Mom started dating this guy several months after your death, I was distraught.

I know I told you he has big, white teeth. You can't miss them when he smiles, and I don't say that as a compliment. The thing is, Dad, I saw early on how this sneaky, smiley man would interact with our family and his.

Many times, I would notice his smile slowly disappear.

I began to see that he was actually a "not-so-smiley" man. He'd lob insults at Mom and I she wouldn't do or say anything. She'd just take it!

I saw how he was with his own family. It was nothing like how we were when we were all together.

I know our family is not perfect—Gram and Grampie constantly yell at each other in German; you and Mom would yell a lot; Grandma and Grandpa Hogan didn't yell, but they also never talked to each other.

But, Dad, this guy is different. He can sometimes say things that sting like direct missiles to the heart. He is mean. I can sense it. I see an emptiness in his eyes, which I think is concerning.

Why does Mom ignore it? Why would she allow this guy to get involved in our lives?

There is something unnatural about the way he acts toward me. I get the feeling that he sees me as competition. Maybe I am? He probably figures Shiloh is easier to manage because she is still so little, and I might be more work. I do want attention from Mom. I'm not getting much, but I figure if I did that wouldn't like it because it would take her attention away from him.

I feel like he is the one winning. He is taking Mom away from Shiloh and me. He is getting her heart and her love, and he doesn't deserve it. He isn't a nice guy, Dad. I just know it. I can feel it.

My instincts tell me to run, but where? I asked Mom to let me live with Grandma, but she said no. I have no choice but to move away.

Mom needs to wake up, but I don't know what I can do to make her. Do you think you can send me a sign?

love, me

Dear Dad,

Well, you might be surprised, but I decided to speak up.

It did not go over very well.

Do you remember when I was in kindergarten and my teacher, Mrs. Kline, scolded me for cutting in line to wash my hands? This is when I first learned that there are rules in this world that we are expected to follow. The problem is that I have always felt like certain rules are dumb. I've always known that I can't give in to things that I see as injustices.

While I probably shouldn't have cut in line in kindergarten, I did learn that it's okay to break certain rules, to sometimes go my own way like you, to try to right wrongs.

So, I decided to trust my gut. I told Mom how I feel about the Dorky Dude. I didn't call him that to her, don't worry. I told her that I didn't think he treated her very nicely or talked to her very nicely. I told her that even though he flashes that big smile of his, it seems like it is put on, like he wants you to think he is nice when he really isn't.

I told her that I felt like he didn't want her to give me any attention, that maybe he didn't like having a pre-teen around and was nicer to Shiloh—like he could win her over but knew he couldn't ever win me over. I told her I thought she was making a big mistake moving us in with him and leaving our home in Reese. I told her that things were hard enough without having to start at a new school and make new friends.

And guess what? Mom didn't even look miffed or annoyed with me. In time, I trust the truth will come out and she will see what I see. My instincts have always been good to me.

I don't get it, Dad, even if she thought what I said was wrong or out of line, she could have tried to make me feel like things would be okay. She didn't even do that!

Mom doesn't make any effort to talk with me. She avoids any conversation that might be hard. She's just taking whatever she can get, like the Dorky Dude. She doesn't question whether it's good or bad. Or maybe she doesn't care about anyone else but herself.

I don't care anymore.

I stood up for myself. But I was invisible. And I know you can't make someone see you if they won't.

I know or want to believe she loves me in her own way, it's just not a comforting way. Maybe she just left all the comforting and love up to you, so now I have to do without. The only time she talks to me is to nag me about making my bed, mowing the lawn, unloading the dishwasher, or dusting the furniture.

Knowing how Mom ignored what I shared with her about the Dorky Dude makes me both angry and sad, but I also know I still have my inner voice—that voice you taught me to listen to, to depend on to give me courage to ride up those sand dunes. It's not always easy to hear it now that you are gone, but I'm trying really hard to since I know that is what you'd tell me to do.

Thinking about our family memories helps me. I know that things felt good and right in our lives, and I have to remember those times in order to get through this time.

I feel happy when I think of all the fun times we spent with Mom's family—like the holiday traditions, times spent at Drummond Island, or at the gravel pit Grampie bought and built. I also remember eating calico beans and roasted pig with the apple in its mouth.

On your side of the family, it was always Grandpa's and Grandma's farmhouse that was the most special. Being with Grandma Rosie was always my favorite thing to do. Maybe I will name my inner voice Rosie, after Grandma.

I am listening to my inner feelings, Dad. These inner guides have always helped me when I've needed help the most. I turned to them when I needed to find my way through the woods when I was little, and when the butterflies in my stomach were so bad that I couldn't eat anything at the church gathering after your funeral.

Knowing that Mom doesn't care how I feel, and we *are* going to live with the Dorky Dude, I will have to really concentrate and listen to my inner voice more than ever. I think you would be proud of me for realizing that.

love, me

Dear Dad,

I want you to know I am okay. I am finding some solace (excellent word choice, right?) in family and food.

Food makes me think of Grandma Rosie. Then, second in line would be Great Gram and Grampie, on Mom's side of the family. The older I get, the more I see what a great guardian and gatekeeper Gram is. She has a way about her. She is both soft and strong. She always smells like baby powder and Estee Lauder perfume. And she always wears that delicate pink apron when she's in the kitchen, but you can't let those girlie things fool you. The way she kneads that dark, molasses-looking Lebkuchen dough proves how strong she is.

I think Gram is the only person who can yell at me and still make me feel loved.

One thing I don't get is how Gram and Grampie have gotten along for over fifty years. Maybe Gram just got used to Grampie barking orders at everyone around him. Uncle Dane once said, "He is a stout German." I am not sure what that means.

Gram and Grampie definitely have an odd relationship... a dichotomy of power. I got the word "dichotomy" right at this year's spelling bee.

They swear at each other in German and often seem very different, but still family oriented. We all still gather in that rugged and rustic log cabin on the lake in Drummond Island, near Canada.

Every summer we'd watch Wimbledon first thing in the morning while eating waffles. I still get bugged by the pools of sticky syrup that Cousin Ryan dribbles all over the pine picnic table.

I hope to continue to go every summer, even when I'm a teenager. I don't want to miss it.

It's hard to think that the Dorky Dude might start joining us. It will be awful if he does. These are *our* family traditions, and the Dorky Dude doesn't have any place in them.

Everything we do has been done for years. I don't think Cousin Perry would want the Dorky Dude there, either.

I wonder if he could not invite him.

Gram once told me there are things in life I can control, and things outside my control.

I am now beginning to truly understand and live with what this means.

There are so many things that are outside of my control— your death, Mom's lack of love and attention, being Shiloh's parent, Mom's new love interest, and now having to move from the only home and people I know and love.

For my thirteenth birthday, I got a pink kneeboard from Grandpa Jim. It only took me two tries to pull myself out of the water, tuck my knees, and balance on the board. With a little help from Cousin Perry, I was doing tricks on Lake Huron in no time: 360 spins, wake jumps, and ollies. If you were there, you would have had such a big smile on your face.

Being with family makes me happy. Even though I miss you, spending time with Grandma Rosie or going up to the lake with Gram and Grampie helps to fill the void I have in my heart. I don't know what I'd do if Mom messes with this part of our life, too.

So many good memories are made up at the lake every summer. I have all the ones I made with you, and now all the new ones I can add to them. Maybe I will eventually feel whole again.

The mystery and magic of Drummond Island will remain in my heart forever, just like you, Dad.

love, me

Dear Dad,

I can squirm my way out of a lot of things, like getting out of chores or confessing to some mischief, but I'm not going to be able to squirm out of moving away from Reese.

It's late so I can't write you a very long letter, but I have to tell you that it's happening, and it scares me. Moving away from our home makes me feel like I'm being taken away from you. I want to make sure you know where I'll be so that you can still hear me.

My relationship with Mom is even worse than before. I never had the same connection with Mom as I did with you, but I didn't feel totally disconnected from her like I do now. She never tells me that she loves me. Maybe she thinks I am unlovable. Maybe I remind her of you. I really have no idea.

What I do know is leaving Reese scares me because I might lose my connection to both you and Grandma by being so far away. I cry thinking about you and not being able to visit your grave.

I can hear Mom in her room next door. She's talking on the phone with her *fiancé*. She's giggling and sounding so happy. I want to be happy for her, but she is destroying my life. I will never understand why things have happened the way they have. I want answers. I'll keep writing to you, Dad. Just know that it won't be from Reese.

love, me

Dear Dad,

Living in Hemlock is awful.

Mom's Dorky Dude doesn't have a warm bone in his body. We moved in with him and I feel like we've been kidnapped and are now living in a post-medieval prison.

His family is always agitated about something. All they do is scream and fight... literally fistfight, Dad. He and his brothers throw punches at each other, even on holidays. It's pure insanity and leaves me speechless. I sometimes look at Mom and think, *I saw this coming, how did you, not?*

Before moving here, Shiloh and I went with Mom to Hemlock to "celebrate" Christmas with the Dorky Dude's family. Shiloh went to play with his niece in the bedroom. Somehow, this purple, sponge-like cartoon character and water from it dripped onto a velvet dress the little girl had lying on her bed. Her mother, Dorky Dude's sister, went whacko.

The whole thing seemed so nuts. I couldn't understand why a little water caused such an explosion. Mom, Shiloh, and I all stood in shock.

It was obvious that day that Dorky Dude has a very defensive and short-tempered family. I wanted to leave and go back home to Reese and never return. I told that to Mom, but she ignored my feelings again, and we went ahead and moved.

So that proves she doesn't care what I think.

I am not even sure this guy's family realizes they are so angry. I asked Mom why she thought they all sparked so easily. She said that they are trustworthy, even though it doesn't always appear that way. That made no sense to me.

Living away from Grandma and all my memories is painful. I barely get to talk to Grandma Rosie on the phone, and I never see any of our relatives on Mom's side. It's like I am now trapped in a prison environment without a key, powerless to escape the storm of emotions that erupt frequently around me. I am still processing my own from your death and moving away from my home and people that loved me better than this family.

We are now living in Dorky Dude's A-frame Tudor on a street called Spencer Drive. It has a long driveway, a pitched roof, and dark-framed windows. It's painted a brown color that I swear I will never paint anything in my life because I want to erase this house and its color forever.

I'm expected to shovel the endlessly long driveway in the winter. No one ever asked or told me that would be the case. It just is. At least he has a snowblower to make it a little easier.

And yes, I'm expected to mow the lawn that surrounds the house like a national park; it takes at least two hours or more. No one told me this either

I miss Reese.

Mom wants me to call Vicar Barber. She thinks I am angry and mean to Dorky Dude or maybe I should call him Demon Dude. She thinks Vicar can get through to me. We are living in hell. Maybe I'll share that with Vicar and see how Mom likes it. Maybe he can explain to Mom that my new stepfather's consistent negative and verbal abuse has forced me to develop a defensive attitude as a means of self-protection, to protect myself emotionally, maybe Mom should try it. How am I supposed to respect this guy, Dad, when he has been nothing but disrespectful and harmful. I respond with nastiness too as a form of retaliation and really just to undermine his authority. Gram calls it teenage rebellion, and me asserting my independence, well she also wrote in my birthday card, "Be nice to your mother" and proceeded to scribble how I have the devil in me. How does one deal with that?

I won't poke the bear if the bear doesn't come after me or my sister. Mom is on her own. She chose this for herself, I did not.

Seeing how nasty he and his family are makes me think of what I want and what I don't want in the future. Someday, I hope to be as cool of a parent as you were. I want to recreate the feelings I felt with you, Grandma Hogan, and Mom's family. But now that we live far away from them, I feel like they are going to forget us and that I may lose how they made me feel and think of myself. We are now isolated from all of them.

Dad, what is crazy is no one thinks this man that mom married is a problem. I guess no one really knows him. Grandma Rosie and the rest of the family probably think we all went off to live happily ever after. Funny how that is, right?

We only hang out with Demon Dude's family now.

I've learned to mask my feelings and put up a giant wall around me. Basically, I try to disguise the numbness I feel. Otherwise, it would all be too overwhelming to bear. Allowing numbness to take over seems to be the only way to get through the next four years. I need to move out and make my own money. Thank you for still being here for me, Dad.

love, me

Dear Dad,

It's weird to think I'm in high school now. It feels like time moved forward, yet I stood still. I'm older but I still carry so much sadness, sorrow, and disbelief for how Mom, Shiloh and I now live.

My high school is in a town called Saginaw. It's twenty-eight minutes away so I have to carpool with this older group of kids every day, both going and returning, unless I have some after-school activity. It's absolutely a-w-f-u-l.

But hey, Mom is happy. I think.

She must like feeling under siege to his unpredictable wrath. I don't and will remind her and him of it, which more often than not, gets me grounded. Oh well.

Stephanie, a senior I ride with makes me get out at red lights and flick the windshield wipers whenever ice collects on them. She's friendly, though, and always drinks a Big Gulp from 7-11 every morning. Sometimes, I'll use my lunch money and buy a bag of chips when we make that stop.

School is routine, but the food is pretty good.

Playing sports after school has been a lifesaver. The downfall is my mother's new husband (still Demon Dude), often drives me home because he works nearby.

Demon Dude is an intense guy. When he comes to my games, especially my basketball games, he critiques every play I made as we drive home, and then makes me practice my jump shots and dribbling in the driveway until almost ten at night.

He works for a company as a union contractor. He has an office that he goes to in Saginaw, but also works in the field. Both his dad and his brother work for this same company. It seems like he gets a lot of perks and makes a good living.

Despite the drama of living with this guy, Mom seems to like that she lives comfortably.

I would be okay with all that if I hadn't found out that Demon Dude wasn't actually the big caretaker he was pretending to be. Though I shouldn't have been snooping through Mom's stuff, I needed money to buy dinner after one of my games and Mom wouldn't give it to me. So, I decided to sneak it from her check-book. She always keeps a stash of bills in there. When I opened her checkbook, I saw the register and noticed that she's been depositing all your social security checks into their bank account. So, basically, she was helping pay our way living with Demon Dorky Dude. She was supposed to be saving those checks in a college fund for me and Shiloh. I no longer trust him or her.

I've tried to like my stepfather, but he always makes it so difficult. He had been married before Mom, but never had kids, so I get that suddenly having two kids might not be easy. I can tell he is unsure about what his role should be, especially with me. I was already fourteen when he and Mom got married, and Shiloh was seven.

I know Shiloh probably misses you, but she was still little when you died, and she needs a daddy. I don't need or want any-one to take your place. It's not the way I'd like for you to be in my life, but I feel good connecting with you through my letters.

Living in captivity, Dad, with someone whose anger dictates everybody's moves and thoughts is not a walk in the park.

love, me

Dear Dad,

My room has become my sanctuary. It's on the second floor and has paisley blue wallpaper with a country-heart-looking border. Mom and my stepfather (look at me being nice) got me an oak four-drawer desk, a five-drawer chest, and a full-size bed with a dark wood headboard. Shiloh's room is down the hall. The two of us share a bathroom, though I am expected to clean it every Saturday.

I was invited to go to Homecoming this year by a senior guy named Joel. I would have liked to have gone, but Mom wouldn't let me because she said that a freshman is too young to go with a senior.

Joel is a warmhearted guy with blue eyes. He wrote me a long letter and included the lyrics of the song "A Groovy Kind of Love" by Phil Collins. It felt really nice to get that letter, like I was being seen and loved. I made the mistake of telling Mom, and she said I was too young to understand.

I disagree. I think it's her who doesn't understand love. Demon Dude does *not* love her and treats us poorly. I am seeing the pattern of him liking to control Mom, and me.

What I'm about to share with you will sound like I'm complaining, but I'm not. I totally understand that chores are required, whether we live here or in Reese. It's always been a requirement in our family to help out, but it's extreme here— next level crazy.

I would guess that for most girls my age there would be certain required chores—like setting the table, cleaning my room, vacuuming, dusting, and loading/unloading the dishwasher. But those are just the basics of living in this house!

Seriously, Dad, this guy is nuts. Shiloh and I do *all* the lawn chores and more! There's an entire acre of property to care for. I have to do the heavy lifting, which means way more.

Since Shiloh can't operate a mower, she helps cut the lawn with scissors. She takes these kitchen scissors and goes to each tree in the yard, no matter how small or large, and trims the blades that the push mower can't get to. Yes, Dad, you read that right.

I circle each tree with the manual push mower first, and then Shiloh does the final trimming. The height of each blade of grass needs to be even around each tree or all hell will break loose. There are over twenty trees in the yard.

After Shiloh finishes up her job of trimming around all the trees with her shears, I finish up the rest of the lawn with the riding mower, which takes another hour. I wear these cumbersome work boots because I'm scared of snakes. I told Demon Dude this, and he didn't care. So far, I have seen three, but they just slithered away. Gross.

The situation here is horrible. You would be so mad if you knew all the chores they make us do. You'd probably come back from the dead and haunt him if you could.

I am beginning to understand why this man married my mom. He needed "helpers" to maintain his house!

Life here is awful, but I am learning a lot about myself as a result. I think you would be proud of me. I have learned that I will not allow the tensions or tempers of grown men to scare me. Mom's new husband and all the other men in his family use anger and yelling to try to get their way, but I don't allow them to frighten me.

I can see how dangerous men can get, but I have learned to not have a fear response since that is what they want. I look them all directly in the eyes, especially the Dorky Demon Dude and his father.

I don't know how I have gained this strength. I'd like to think it's because you are here with me, like you are my armor, helping me move toward the enemy without fear.

Maybe I was born with bravery, like you. I don't remember you fearing anything in life. Maybe you feared death, or leaving me, Mom, and Shiloh. I never witnessed your fear, though.

I'm pretty sure that the Demon Dude knows I don't like him, and I won't fear him, and that is why he punishes me.

love, me

Dear Dad,

Drama plays daily in this house.

It's tiring, it's annoying, and it's disturbing.

However, high school life keeps me distracted which is a good thing.

Being a sophomore is cool. I ride into school almost every day with a guy named Todd, who is one year older than me. He's easygoing and always lets me change the radio station to whatever I want to listen to. Maybe it's Todd's personality, or the fact that I'm a year older, but the drive this year is easier. He has pretty bad acne, which makes mine not seem so terrible.

I've made some new friends. They distract me from everything going on at Dorky Dude's house.

My new friends are Kathy, Becky, Kelly, and Amy. They are all great and all very different.

I met Kathy at a summer basketball clinic before freshman year. We were both moved up to the Junior Varsity (JV) basketball team that year after tryouts. We play on the Varsity Volleyball and Varsity Softball teams together now. She lives on a pig farm. I was there once and gagged from the stench of those pigs.

Becky lives in a beautiful house and has two golden retrievers. We have the best time together. I like sleeping over at her house, not only to get away from the one I live in, but because it's always so much fun. If we aren't making cinnamon rolls and sipping fresh squeezed orange juice, we're hanging out in her room singing Milli Vanilli's songs. Also, Becky has the best clothes. We pretend that we are fashion designers and style each other in clothes from her closet.

My friend Kelly is a wild one. We probably connect the most. I can be my complete self with her. We love making puppy chow snack mix and eating the entire batch. It's so good. We do this funny dance when we make it—jumping around and shaking the Chex mix in a brown grocery bag. One time, I told her dad that doctors suck. He looked at me with this quizzical expression and asked why. I told him none of them could save you. I think I might have surprised him with my answer. I'm not sure he knew that you had died. Once he heard my answer, though, he said he agreed with me completely.

I really like Kelly's dad, Mr. Sendtko. I think you would like him, too, Dad. He looks like Santa, with the same teddy-bear personality and warm smile, but without the white hair and beard.

Amy is my most brilliant friend and probably the most excellent person I have ever met. I really like her, even though we don't have a lot of the same interests. She babysits a lot. That's one thing we definitely don't have in common. Babysitting is not for me. I've had my fill, thank you very much. Both of Amy's parents are educators and in school administration in a different district than the one we attend. Even though we are different, I like hanging out with her and chilling at her house. It's always quiet, nobody yells, and it has a calm energy, unlike Dorky Dude's house.

Sometimes, the five of us will get together, but that doesn't always go well. I think that while I find I have a strong connection with each of them individually, the group connection doesn't always work. It seems like one of those girls will always get upset about something. I don't ever really get bothered by the same things, but I suppose that's because chaos is a constant in my life. Silly girl drama is nothing in comparison.

love, me

Dear Dad,

School and my friends continue to keep me sane. Basketball has been my greatest savior. I'm so thankful you taught me how to play. You gave me the fundamentals early on. It's not only active and challenging, but it's given me a social outlet, a way to connect with my peers that's easier for me. And it's made me love sports in general.

I like to push myself to be better.

I am learning a lot about myself competing athletically. Sometimes, I can get fiery, which I think is good. Coach Brandt said that this was a good quality of mine, but that I need to learn to channel it better. I understand what he's saying, and I am working on it.

I do wish I'd had more time with you. You would have taught me so much more. I played a lot after you died but I could have used more lessons from you. My dribbling could be better, but my jump shot is pure.

I'm pretty scrappy on the court and I like chasing the ball. Defense is my specialty.

Having a lot of energy to "channel" (Coach Brandt's word, not mine)—or maybe the pure frustration I feel from living with Dorky Dude— can get in the way at times. It can be distracting and mess with my game. But I work hard, and Coach Brandt told the crowd at the awards banquet that I am tenacious. I like thinking that it shows that I won't relinquish or give up.

These are the moments that keep me sane, Dad.

Sometimes, I wonder how I don't lose it. I guess I "channel" more than I thought. I think of you and Grandma Rosie (who I miss like crazy), and I visualize us all together again. This brings me peace inside.

love, me

Dear Dad,

Junior year, unfortunately, has posed some problems for me. I don't have as much time to write to you as I used to.

My basketball season was cut short. I tore my ACL during the second quarter of our team's game against Swan Valley. It was such a random accident. I had gone in for a rebound. When I came down with the ball, my foot landed on top of the defender's foot, causing me to twist my ankle and fall to the court.

My coach immediately took me out of the game, but I convinced him to let me warm up during halftime to show him I could still play. After shooting a few practice shots, I was told to sprint to half court and back. The minute I pivoted and changed direction I heard a popping sound, and I fell back down. Only this time, I couldn't get up on my own.

In short, I had to have two surgeries: one orthoscopic surgery, followed by a major reconstructive surgery on my knee. I will say that this was the one and only time that I saw my stepfather in a good light. I guess it pays to know people because he managed to secure a prominent orthopedic surgeon in Detroit to do both surgeries. I was in good hands. And it was cool to find out that this doc had worked with hockey players from the Detroit Red Wings.

I ended up getting a job at McDonald's to fill some of my time. You know me, I can't just sit around. Being unable to play basketball was devastating, though.

Thankfully, I had met someone and was dating him at that same time.

He kind of kept me from being totally depressed about my injury.

My boyfriend's name is Jared. He's a golf guy (I know you would like that) and on the Varsity team. He also has a great tan. In fact, his sun-kissed skin matches mine.

I am definitely attracted to Jared, so I know I overlook how different we are. I'm sassy, and he's stiff and strict. We started off hanging out in a group with some mutual friends but eventually went alone together to the movies. I can honestly say that I didn't end up seeing many of the scenes in *The Dead Poets Society* that day, and Robin Williams is one of my favorite actors. What I did end up with is chapped lips from making out with Jared. We were pretty much together as a couple after that.

Anyway, Jared is really polite and has beautiful, piercing, hazel green eyes. And he dresses like a golfer in Polo shirts and shorts almost every day. I like him, but I wonder a little about our differences in personality.

It's too early to tell if that's good or bad. I sometimes think we might be a little like you and Mom.

I have had a few other boyfriends, but none that have meant enough to me to write about. It's funny, but there was another

Jared, before this one. He was two years older and gave me his class ring.

Mom said I had to return it, but I hid it in the bathroom basket of fake flowers, and she found it. So, I did end up giving it back.

The only other one I'll mention is Jim, a counselor at Camp Lu Lay Lea. I met him at the camp the summer after you died. He was really nice, but to be honest, I think it was all the fun activities we did that summer that attracted me to him. I needed a distraction and activities to fill my brain and body so I could have a break from the sadness that filled me up the rest of the time.

What I have realized in every interaction I've had with "potential" boyfriends is that I am constantly looking for stability. I need someone to count on.

All through high school, I've lived in a completely dysfunctional, chaotic household with no stability whatsoever. As I spent more time with Jared, I found his family to be the kind of family I want to have. They are kind, caring, welcoming, and nice to each other.

Even though I realize that my ying-yang relationship with Jared was maybe not the best match, I ignore that because his family feels like the life preserver I so desperately need right now. They provide a safe place to be and to think, away from the craziness of living with the Dorky Dude.

It's not like I didn't try to get along with him in the beginning. I was polite and pleasant. Honestly, I was. I obeyed his rules and followed his directions on managing all he asked of me—his endless list of chores and his ridiculous pickiness on how to do them. I even cleaned his twenty-one-foot Liberator boat each and every time it was used.

I came to realize that Dorky Dude wanted to treat me the way he felt inside. It's like rage just lives inside him, so rage comes out. Like he can't get out of his own way, so he gets in mine.

I know that I can feel anger, too, but the difference is I know how to change lanes, and he doesn't.

All those anger issues we experienced early on with Demon Dude's family have continued.

I have seen the look on Mom's face during these blowups. She knows this isn't the way we should live. But we remain.

Once when we all went up to Dorky Dude's family lake house, he got in a screaming match with his younger brother Ernie.

They were all the way on the other side of the lake and Mom, Shiloh, and I could hear them from our paddle boats on the opposite shore. Those types of altercations are the norm with that family.

I should have known that it was just a matter of time before Dorky Dude would lose control of his rage and it would affect Mom, Shiloh, or me. I feel bad telling you about this, but I can't keep everything bottled up inside me. It's hard to write about, but it's even harder to suppress.

I can't help Mom if she doesn't want to help herself. All I can try to do is protect Shiloh and myself. Shiloh is still too young to figure out how to respond to this guy. I do my best to be there for my little sister, but I am barely getting by myself.

I've found that ignoring the Dorky Dude is effective. I don't get mixed up in his rage, and I don't cower away. I know he doesn't like it, but there's nothing for him to grab on to and pull me into the chaos if I won't bite.

Poor guy just keeps getting suffocated by his own anger. I get it but try not to let his or my own imprison me—that's where we are different.

Most of the time, when Dorky Dude grounds me, he will take me off the car insurance.

I laugh every time because all that happens is he has to drive me to school, which he hates. You see, he can't get out of his own way.

love, me

Dear Dad,

It's been a while since I've written. Finishing up high school was a whirlwind. You'll be happy to know that after months of physical therapy and wearing a bionic brace, I was able to play basketball, volleyball, and softball my senior year. Unfortunately, because I missed a good bit of playing, I also missed out on a chance for a basketball scholarship at a community college.

I figure life has other plans for me.

Maybe the biggest news of my senior year has nothing to do with school. Mom and Dorky Dude had a baby!

Brinley Jo was born on December 11th. I helped name her.

My favorite cartoon character from Alvin and the Chipmunks is the little girl with the ponytail, yellow scarf, and leg warmers. She's the one that inspired me to wear leg warmers outside of dance class. I thought that was so cool!

Anyway, the little girl's name is Brinley Miller. She's seen as the cutest and cleverest of the group, and a bit bossy. I like that my sister will share that name. Her middle name, Jo, comes from the first two letters in Mom's name, Joni.

Even though I love Brinley Jo, or BJ, as we liked to call her, I don't know how Dorky Dude is going to be as a father.

I've come to think of him as a particular guy. I liken him to Martin in "Sleeping with the Enemy." In that movie, Martin's wife resorts to faking her death in an attempt to escape her life with him. After years of abuse and being forced to live in an unacceptable situation, she realizes her plan is the only way she can flee Martin's control.

My life with Dorky Dude has been eerily similar to that movie. Even though I'm not the one married to him, I've had to deal with all his bizarre behaviors and his abusive rage. And, like Julia Robert's character, I feel like there's no way out.

Dorky Dude aka Martin has some horrible human qualities.

I've tried for years to tell Mom that his behavior is wrong. Abusive is really the right word. But she never listens. So, now they have Brinley . I like her a lot.

My newest little sister loves to sing. From the time she could walk, she'd parade around the kitchen with a wooden spoon, pretending it was her microphone.

When Brinley was about a year old, things got really bad.

It was Super Bowl Sunday and he was watching the game and chomping on his popcorn. Mom, Shiloh, BJ, and I were in the kitchen. Mom was cutting Shiloh's hair, and I was watching our little superstar performer as she toddled around singing into her wooden spoon microphone. As BJ made her way around the room, her spoon accidentally knocked against one of the cupboards.

Within seconds, he came stomping into the kitchen and snatched the wooden spoon out of BJ's little hand. Her eyes immediately welled up with tears. He tossed the spoon onto the counter and returned to his game, never saying a word. As soon as he left the room, I gave the spoon back to Brinley.

Maybe he was bugged because his team was losing that day, or perhaps he just has no internal barometer to control his inner rage. Any petty annoyance gets the same response as a major grievance. And, truly, nothing I've witnessed in my time with him would warrant any of the responses he has had.

I do wonder if that man ever visited a therapist. He has an insane preoccupation with rules, order, organization, and schedules. His verbal assassination of everyone around him is way over the top.

Growing up in constant turmoil is not good, Dad. I know that. I've lived it. The only good that has come from this loneliness is it has taught me to be courageous, to love myself when no one else will. This is what saved me that day.

When I saw him raging toward me, I knew I needed to get away. I ran down the long hallway, heading for the stairs as fast as my feet could take me. I was only halfway up when he grabbed my left ankle. He dragged me to the landing below. When I managed to get my balance, I looked directly into his evil eyes.

I didn't think anything could scare me as much as your death, Dad, but Martin's darkness is different. There's a malice in him that disturbing in a wild wicked way that I don't have words to describe.

No amount of fighting back would have changed the outcome of your death. I had no control over that. But this? This I needed to fight.

With him towering over me, I launched into verbally assaulting him as best I could, while looking directly into his snake-like eyes.

I had no fear, Dad.

He grabbed me around the neck. I managed to break free twice, but he grabbed ahold of me and forced me toward the stained-glass window to the right of the storm door. I braced myself against the doorframe and managed to grab hold of the door handle, pushing the door open before he could push me through it. He lost his hold, and I was able to break free. I ran as fast as I could, barefoot through the snow to the neighbors.

Colleen, our closest neighbor, opened the door and let me in. I immediately called Jared. His mom answered the phone, saying he was watching the game with his dad at Dr. Sheen's, but she would try to reach him. I called Uncle Dane next. I'm sure Colleen was confused seeing me in basketball shorts, a T-shirt, and no shoes, wondering what was going on.

As I waited to get picked up, I could hear Mom screaming at her husband to stop and Shiloh sobbing. I wondered what was happening, but I couldn't go back. That would only make things worse. It broke my heart to leave Shiloh, but I had to protect me in that moment.

All this transpired because I gave my one-year-old half-baby-sister a wooden spoon to use as a microphone!

Jared picked me up within thirty minutes. Uncle Dane was waiting in Jared's driveway when we pulled up.

I don't think I've ever seen Uncle Dane so mad. Since he's a Michigan State Police Trooper, he knows the importance of evidence. He took pictures of the bruises forming on my neck and ankle. He wanted to approach mom's husband right then and there, but I begged him not to because I feared what that might do to Mom and Shiloh.

A day or two later, Uncle Dane and I returned to Spencer Road so I could get some of my things. Mom had told Aunt Kay that she and Dorky Dude both would be at work. She also told Aunt Kay that right after the blowup, the Dorky Dude had taken almost all my belongings from my room and thrown them out onto the front lawn. When Mom and Shiloh gathered everything up and returned it to my room, he did it again the next night! So, Mom and Shiloh gathered and returned everything yet again, and that was that. I guess he figured he'd made his point. I was out of there! Even though I worried about Mom, I'm also furious with her.

She allowed this man to manipulate her, to be mean to Shiloh, to bully his one-year-old daughter to tears, and to attempt to beat the shit out of me. I was done fighting for her. I didn't care anymore. I didn't have the energy for it.

I did care for Shiloh, but I could not be her mother anymore. I had to try to mother myself.

Mom and I did not speak during those months I lived away. I was deeply affected by what had happened, but I managed to keep myself together, play volleyball, and complete my homework.

Though I know you are probably livid with what Mom's husband did, I also know you are proud of how I defended myself and got away.

love, me

Dear Dad,

I was nominated to be on Homecoming Court. Crazy me, right? Your tomboy, who you said would never be a "runway model" because of all the scars on my legs from falling off my bike and other silly stuff we did.

I was shocked. I didn't know how to respond when they announced it over the speaker system. I was excited on the inside but controlled my outside feelings.

Jared has been making me feel bad because I was nominated when he wasn't. He's been making comments about me not being more considerate of his feelings of not being chosen.

I told him to fuck off.

That wasn't the right thing to say, but it's not my job to keep making everyone feel good about themselves.

What about me? When do I get to feel good?

Anyway, he's the least of my problems right now. I like his family but don't want to be with him anymore. I feel trapped and not sure how to break up with him. I want his family's support right now.

Is this wrong, Dad? I feel scattered and spinning. I wish you were here. I know you would help me solve everything or just make it disappear.

love, me

Dear Dad,

Living at Aunt Kay's and Uncle Dane's house has been weird. I'm grateful they took me in, but I don't belong here or anywhere, really.

Life has unleashed so much on me that has been difficult to figure out. There has been so much grief, loneliness, and turmoil. And yet, I am proud of how I've managed to pull myself through the hard times. I found the strength to believe in myself and keep truckin' along.

While losing you was the most painful event in my life, it required me to work hard in handling my emotions—to be smart and strategic in order to get through. I'm proud of myself, Dad.

I still have anger and resentment issues, but I think my ability to recognize this in light of all you taught me about being aware of my surroundings, not fearing failure, and trusting my gut, helped me maintain my self-control when faced with challenge. I never once acted like Mom's husband or his family. Although, I have been mean to Shiloh at times, maybe I should tell her I am sorry and am struggling myself.

Sports allowed me to diffuse my resentment and channel my pent-up energy. And this was super helpful, but sports, socializing with friends, and doing all my chores have never been enough. I realize that when I lost you—and Mom didn't step up—I lost my stability, my protector, and the only person I felt loved me uncon-ditionally. Life changed dramatically after you died. I had to grow up much quicker than was fair. I feel much older than I am.

I long for more, Dad. I would like someone to support me.

Is this corny?

I still miss Grandma and the comfort of consistency that she provided. I did make friends, and I have Jared and his family, but I crave a greater sense of belonging.

While I know there is still a void within me, and anger and resentment that I'll have to wade through, I do know that living in that home on Spencer Road is hell and not something I'm okay with.

Eventually, after a month or so at Aunt Kay's and Uncle Dane's, Mom tried to get in touch with me. I wasn't ready so it took a few conversations with Aunt Kay before I agreed to talk to Mom. We met in her car at Freeway Fritz's while Aunt Kay waited.

Mom looked desperate. She said that "her Martin" was sorry and wanted me to return.

I know Mom must have gotten the brunt of punishment for my behavior. I did feel for her. I have, of course, never talked to her about this, but I sense it's probably what happened. Martin had to unleash his rage on someone, and I certainly wasn't there.

Mom never apologized. She just told me that it was okay to come back because her Martin was sorry. But whatever. It's not like that was totally surprising. I always find myself wishing Mom might finally do or say something to show me she cares about me, but she never does.

I did go back, Dad, to the fortress of anger on Spencer Road. It was against my better judgment. I went back for Shiloh, not so much for Mom. I was still really mad at Mom.

When I walked back into the house after having been at Aunt Kay's and Uncle Dane's, Mom told me to go directly to my room and not say anything or do anything. I thought that was kind of strange, since she told me that Martin was sorry. But I headed in that direction, minding what she said. Before I got a few steps in, the shit hit the fan.

The minute Martin set his demonic eyes on me he started yelling at me. I locked my eyes on him and continued toward the stairs to my room.

I felt betrayed by Mom because it was obvious that her Martin *wasn't* sorry. He didn't want me there.

I wasn't going to let him have any power over me. I never said anything or physically reacted to him. I just stared directly into his gunmetal eyes and did not flinch. He did not like that.

Everything pretty much blew up after that. Martin told Mom that it was him or me and when Mom didn't respond to him, he took off for his parents' house. Of course, he didn't just walk out, he stormed out, knocking things off the wall, kicking anything his foot could reach, and slamming his fist against doors and walls as he exited. As always, his rage was over the top.

love, me

Dear Dad,

After an intervention with Uncle Dane and Grandpa Bernthal, Grandpa's lawyer told Martin to stay out of the house while things were sorted. Little did he know that divorce was the goal.

I would like to think Mom admittedly got scared and maybe tired of Martin's expectations, like stacking the heavy loads of wood delivered in the backyard and not lifting a finger to help Mom and I. Beyond taking advantage of Mom, he demeaned her. He called her Belly Jo, referring to the extra weight she gained and had trouble losing after giving birth to Brinley Jo.

Mom has a huge heart. I think it's too big. She is friendly and lets a lot of people take advantage of her. Well, you know this too, Dad.

She told me some things lately about your drinking problem. It was a little out of character for her, but I think she told me because she was feeling attacked by me. Whatever the reason, you and I can discuss that later. The best and biggest blowup occurred when Mom "finally" served divorce papers after four and a half long years of living together. After a couple of weeks, he showed up at the house along with his mom and dad. Mom, Shiloh, Brinley , and I had just gotten home from my senior high school banquet and there they all were in the driveway.

As soon as we all got into the house, verbal warfare was launched. I was holding Brinley Jo at the time and in the middle of all the yelling from these three crazy people, Martin's dad walked over to me and forcefully grabbed Brinley Jo from my arms.

He looked me in the eyes as he took her from me and said, "You are not a fucking homecoming queen. You are a fucking piece of shit. Rot in hell."

I already knew how disgusting the Demon Dude and his family were, but when someone targets the poison arrow directly into your heart, it hurts. Those derogatory remarks were said to demean, degrade, and intimidate me. Adding to the hurt is the fact that Mom said nothing.

She stood there and allowed that horrible man to not only roughly grab Brinley , but to speak to me in the most horrific way.

Once they had their say, they left, leaving Brinley crying in Mom's arms, Shiloh scared and me, telling Mom it's time to leave for once and all. It was out a movie, outrageous and nasty—not normal behavior, but again when has this family ever demonstrated nice natural behavior.

I decided at that point, I can't console my mom anymore. But things weren't over. Next began the back and forth—arguing over the settlement of their finances, child support, custody arrangements, etc.

Through all of this I could see Mom losing her will. It was as if she had no fight. I hated to see her weakness in light of how important it was to finally severe her ties to that man.

Instead, I had to be the adult. Mom's lawyer had me help get paperwork needed to finalize divorce documents. It was nuts to me that at eighteen years of age, I had to mother my own mom... again! It was as if we had to "convince" her to divorce this guy.

She let him intimidate her into non-action and things were taking really long to wrap up.

I am losing a lot of respect for Mom. I don't want to, but it has been hard to understand her choices since you died, Dad.

While Martin didn't live with us during this time, his presence was definitely felt. But I was not deterred. I finally felt like we were on the winning side…even if I had to drag Mom over that finish line. Divorce would be the goal!

love, me

The Therapy Sessions
A Note from Tristen

Dear Reader,

Most of us can relate to Shannon's anger. All of us have been required to lift responsibility greater than we should ever have to carry, have been let down by a parent / partner that we love deeply and have masked our feelings to engage in societal norms. We are all wounded adults interpreting the world through the lens of our unmet needs and trauma. Some of us just don't know yet how all of this is interconnected.

Shannon has a desire to be trauma informed. She desperately wants to make sense of the interpersonal relationships that neglected her emotional needs. Her resiliency and desire to know her true self is guiding this stage of therapy.

Understanding trauma is profoundly complicated. And, to be completely transparent, healing trauma is even more intricate and painful. Healing work is brutal. This work takes tremendous guts and profound courage. Shannon has displayed great fearlessness many times in her life. Against all odds, she never gave up.

Our goal is to create a process where her trauma is informing her about what is happening in her inner world. Her complex underground trauma highway in the brain is operating with no lights, no signals, no roadmap. Together we will learn these paths, we will discover a way to shine light, uncover the signals, create a roadmap.

A roadmap to witnessing her own trauma.

As she engages in self-reflection, engages in the work, engages in the evolution of Shannon, she will become more skilled in recognizing trauma activation. This can take years, even a lifetime, to master.

Her environment role modeled insecure attachment, continual conflict, avoidance, and repression of self. Her desire to 'fix' everyone's problems and deep longing for a family feeling promoted her creation of Numbville, her creatively named inner fictional town where one escapes to avoid the distress of life. I want her to not only imagine a world the opposite of Numbville, but to become just as skilled at negotiating an inner world where she can sense, recognize and be informed by trauma. Trauma is meant to teach us. Trauma is meant to inform us.

One day she will learn to recognize it not as an alarm, but as a signal. Rather than responding to trauma by masking, people pleasing, or becoming overly self-protective, she will allow it to just be there, to exist, to be observed. She will learn to pause without reacting as long as she possibly can. Witnessing activation. Knowing it is a protective warning from the past, from her reptilian, old brain attempting to keep her alive.

She will learn to honor this biological warning. And then, she will learn to release trauma triggers without judgment. Therapy works because we are introduced to new ways of thinking about ourselves and our story. Therapy allows us to create new thought patterns in the mind.

All of these together to form new neural pathways in the brain. These processes allow for intense growth and authentic self-alignment.

Isn't that what we all want?

XOXO
Love, Tristen

The Self Betrayal Session
by Tristen

I walk into my office and turn on the lights and spa music. I pour a heavy dose of lavender in the waiting room diffusor and then sit to check my email. Ten minutes later, my lobby light turns red acknowledging her early arrival.

We briefly discuss the rare occurrence of rain we are having, her drive, and the dynamics of back-to-school season. We both understand the overwhelming transition and the increased intellectual gymnastics required of mothers during this time of year. I ask her what her biggest challenge has been in this transition. I am surprised to hear her response.

"I can't tell if my overthinking is helpful," she says.

I cannot help but giggle. I, too, have grappled with this same condition. "There is a part of you that truly believes other people think like you, Shannon. That they see the world through a similar lens. The reality is most people don't," I state calmly. "Assuming that they think like you is destroying your ability to choose wisely. It's misguiding who you trust. It's causing you to pick the wrong people for connection. It's keeping you stuck in Numbville."

"When you refer to your tendency for overthinking," I continue, "you seem proud of it. Like overthinking is a super skill. Honestly, overthinking is linked to clinical anxiety and unresolved fear. Is it possible that to cope with devastating loss, brutal, confusing abandonment, at such a young age, you heavily rely on your intelligence, your intellect to make sense of the world?" I ask lovingly.

"I find that overthinkers tend to be *under-feelers*," I explain. "When you prioritize thinking over feeling, one learns to live more in their brain than in their body. This becomes the default. To over intellectualize our issues, our pain, our people. No one can be in true alignment in overthinking," I say. "Our work is to have your head and heart in alignment, working together to interpret the world, informing you of your entire being's needs. You need to get out of your head and into your body. The next time you notice your default to overthinking, I want you to gently catch the pattern in real time. Lovingly say to yourself, 'Oops! There I go overutilizing my head again. I must be avoiding my feelings.' Then put both hands on your heart and gently press. Feel your heart beating. Feel your aliveness. Ask yourself, 'What am I feeling in my body? What is my system trying to inform me about myself at this time? What do I need to allow myself to feel in this moment?'"

"This process will redirect your limbic system to be more curious about true self safety and self-alignment. Even if for just a few moments you step out of overthinking and into feeling, then our skill is working. Now you just need to do this about a hundred thousand times to create a solid neural pathway."

She smiles knowingly.

"The trouble is you are still prone to emotional vampires. Your subconscious desire to create a family environment that existed before your dad died, that you found as a reprieve with your ex-fiancé's family, is rooted in people pleasing tendencies. If you pour yourself into meeting other's needs, create a wonderful atmosphere, avoid revealing your true self, conceal your anger and resentment. You are simultaneously hiding and suppressing your own needs, while focusing on making others more comfortable. All a giant effort, you make look easy, to feel needed, feel seen, feel connected.

"Here's the thing, Shannon, you are going to have to let people dislike you. You are going to have to disappoint people. This does not define you. The need to be needed is not your life's work. It's your childhood pain projected onto anyone in your proximity who appears to be a stray cat. Stop collecting stray cats! Stop giving yourself away to takers, manipulators, and selfish operators who will suck out your light, your good, your essence and walk away without a second thought to how they've hurt you," I urge.

"Shannon," I continue, "you think you can help them? You think you can save these assholes? Well guess what, you can't save them, and they don't even want to be saved. They love their miserable, conditional, transactional, selfish lives. Who are you to tell them to change and evolve?"

I see the conflict on her face. Her hands clench. Her neck tightens. She doesn't want me to be right.

"You don't need to save anyone but yourself," I tell her. "That isn't your work. It isn't selfish to save yourself. It is an honor to save yourself."

She nods and smiles at me with tears in her eyes. She looks at her many rings and turns a bracelet round and round on her tiny wrist. "Thank you," she says gently.

"It is an honor to see you softening, Shannon," I say with love, my hand over my heart. "I encourage you take a moment in your car to breathe and reflect before you peel off to the next thing." "I will," she says with courageous resolve.

The Inner Voice Session
by Tristen

Shannon walks in with two giant iced black teas and a furrowed brow. She hands me one, kicks off her gold sandals, and cozies into her well-earned spot on my couch. "I want to talk about how I talk to myself, my inner dialogue," she volunteers. She leans back, fluffs a pillow, and stares at me with soft eyes.

"Excellent," I say. "We've talked before about this inner voice of yours. This inner voice is what we call the ego. Our ego is the part of our brain that protects us. It prefers to keep everything the same. The ego is often what we identify as who we *actually* are, our personality really, the *I* and *me*. It is essentially exactly how you see yourself. It is the part of our mind that identifies with our values, our beliefs, our habits, and our styles. The ego is an unconscious part of our mind, an inner voice that we believe guides us and keeps us safe," I inform.

I pause. She drinks from her glistening plastic teacup.

"I find it helpful to name the ego. Naming the ego allows us to separate Shannon from her thoughts, her feelings, and her fears. Can you think of any relevant name for your ego?" I ask.

"Rosie. Rosie is my ego," she states without an ounce of hesitation.

We both knowingly smile. I feel a tug at my heart knowing the deep significance of her paternal grandmother in her life.

"It's the perfect name. Rosie. Rosie is your ego," I validate.

"Rosie is inflexible and prefers to run the show. She is the captain of the ship. Rosie is also very resistant to change. Rosie doesn't like new. Rosie doesn't like different. Rosie doesn't like to be wrong or told what to do." She smiles, she understands.

"In your childhood, Rosie helped you cope. Rosie highlighted your greatest needs. In adolescence, Rosie helped you to advocate for yourself, protect yourself, demand better, stand up to toxic adults. Rosie helped you to find safe friends and families to gravitate toward. In adulthood, Rosie chose Tim—a partner with the skills you needed," I say.

She nods.

"Rosie sees any new ideas as a threat. As something to scrutinize, refuse, reject. Rosie isn't interested in the suggestions of others, including me, your therapist. Rosie tells you that your identity is more important than a new way of thinking, a different way to interpret trauma and a new behavior that helps to heal yourself. Rosie doesn't want you to soften or downgrade her role. She wants to be front and center always," I say calmly. Shannon blinks.

"Rosie has been defending you for a very long time. It is time to lower those defenses."

"Rosie saved me and comforted me and guided me," she says.

I nod knowing it is very true. "Yes, she did. Rosie is a hero. She is not the problem. The problem is you are so enmeshed with Rosie that you have not learned to hear Shannon. Rosie and Shannon must coexist. To determine the best way to evolve, Shannon you must be able to hear both. Rosie can fade into the background and offer more of a mood lighting than a spotlight."

I smile as I see her softening.

"I have no interest in devaluing Rosie. I only want you to learn to trust yourself. I promise you there is room for both of you," I say empathetically. "When you feel triggered, I want you to pause. I want you to ask yourself if you want to pass off these emotions on another person or do you want to allow yourself to experience your own emotions. You deserve to be deeply valued and seen, Shannon. Without the filter of deep hurt and deep abandonment. You deserve to feel safe and to soften your defenses. You are beginning to see that safe people do not want to intentionally hurt, betray, or harm you. This will allow others to come toward you with more ease and more ability to attune to you," I invite.

She nods with a more relaxed understanding.

"I want you to notice when anger shows up. Ask yourself: Is anger helping me grow or stay stuck? Is anger protecting me out of habit when I don't need protecting? Is anger telling me someone or something is unsafe now or is it familiar from the past? Take a breath and learn to investigate. Calmly ask yourself, am I capable of handling this situation? Am I tying my worthiness to the actions of others? Notice and honor the message."

She nods as she looks out the window. She stands up, gives me a grateful hug, and walks out the door with conviction.

The Negative Belief Session
by Tristen

"I'm so pissed," Shannon says while unpacking items from her backpack. Composition books, pens of every color, and multiple sticky notes now cover a majority of my couch. I can see she has clearly taken our journaling exercises to heart. She tosses a few lose pages and gum wrappers into the trash.

This anger has been a pattern. An unsettling rage boiling below the surface. She is resentful of her ability to mask with great skill to blend in. Recreating her adolescence, overly responsible for her sister, her mother, and walking on eggshells in the home of an abusive stepparent. Her profound ability to masterfully turn any environment into one of emotional safety for others, with a low ability to screen people for any capability to give back to her.

Shannon recounts an extended family gathering littered with themes of rigidity, overcompensation, and self-betrayal. All of her current character defaults. I can sense she needs me to assist in deducing these deeply flawed figures, in a selfish family system, with manipulative and mismanaged behaviors. There will be many sessions on narcissistic family systems. Today is the day we address her part in this dynamic. I calmly ask, "Shannon, are you angry at them or at yourself?" She shrugs and grabs a pencil from her messy bun.

"You have meticulously created a mask, perhaps a shield would even be more accurate. The mask presents you as a calm, engaging, inquisitive, capable woman. You are seen as intelligent, likable, beautiful, relaxed. Your mask protects you from being too vulnerable, too revealed. Your mask is a shield, blocking others from seeing your authentic self. Your mask is a trauma response. Prioritizing the comfort of others around you, before prioritizing your needs."

She responds, "I don't relate to any of these people. We don't have anything in common. I don't like small talk. I don't want to complain about everything. I don't want to put down others and pass it off as a joke. I don't want these superficial exchanges."

"What do you want, Shannon?" I ask.

"I want to relate. I want to have deeper conversations. I want to discuss a great character in a book. I want to explore dreams. I want to have vulnerable reflections to digest. I want more depth in my relationships," she says with resolve.

"What do you think is getting in the way of this deeper connection?"

"I don't think most people are capable. I don't think people want to go deep." She states it as factual. "I don't think people know how."

"Perhaps you are right," I agree. "Maybe we are all just adults walking around wounded and afraid that no one will ever understand us or truly see our soul. Maybe we are all just looking for excuses to avoid vulnerability and closeness."

She jots down a note that I will never read.

I continue, "Sometimes emotional closeness is difficult to gain when our early experiences were complicated. You longed as a child to be seen, to be free, to be parented, to be asked how you felt," I point out. "What about the unmet need to be asked if you are willing to take on the responsibility of watching your little sister for a few hours or an entire weekend? That simple gesture would have created consent around your heavy level of responsibility at a very young age," I prompt.

She stares back, quietly reliving those moments embedded in her story.

"Many of our decisions as children are made for us. We didn't even get a chance to verbalize what we need. Over time we learn as children to disregard our own needs and prioritize the comfort of those around us. Over time we learn to internalize our healthy responses to an unhealthy situation and create what are called negative beliefs." She tilts her head, interested.

"Negative beliefs are beliefs developed and formed through small, often unidentifiable seemly insignificant moments, typically in childhood, that keep us separate from others. They are the language of deep wounding that narrates our inner experience and justifies our reasons for choosing aloneness."

She appears more curious after writing one word and circling it .

"Oftentimes negative beliefs develop as we try to make sense of moments that an adult didn't explain to us in a way that resonates. There was a message you gathered from your mom's choices that deeply impacted you. Do you remember how you felt?" I ask.

"Annoyed… mischievous… resentful… free to do what I want… confused," she recounts.

"A giant mixture of conflicting emotions creating uncertainty in your inner world about who you are and what your value is. Negative beliefs are born from these messages we integrate as truths. All of these experiences tether together to create a belief system searching for validation and purpose," I explain. "In therapy we are often interested in identifying what verbal and nonverbal messages were contributing to and helping to create negative beliefs. How did your painful childhood experiences complicate your relationship with self, with your sisters, with your mom, with men throughout your life? What communication challenges, destructive patterns, and negative beliefs did you develop in middle school and high school? How did these beliefs shape the way you see the world? How did you internalize these negative beliefs? What did they teach you about interpersonal relationships and emotional safety? What lessons weren't clear or clarified for you growing up? What can we do to prioritize uncovering this complex set of beliefs and provide more information to clarify the inner dialogue of your story?" I ask.

We digest and dissect the questions.

Shannon continues to make herself notes and circle critical concepts.

"I am going to share a few negative beliefs that I see show up in therapy quite often. Tell me what resonates with you: I am a burden. I am difficult to love. I am not enough. I am invisible. I am alone. I can't trust anyone. I don't feel worthy. I am incapable. I am a failure." We explore the negative beliefs she most relates to.

She insightfully adds others.

"Understanding your negative beliefs and unmet needs requires frequent, meaningful self-check-ins. Each time you feel triggered or dysregulated, I want you to identify the underlying negative belief. This will help us to separate negative beliefs, your ego and your own healthy adult self," I encourage.

She continues to write several thoughts. I observe her formulating.

I patiently listen to the tick tock of my clock. As if she knows what I'm listening to, she looks up, checks the clock and returns her belongings to the backpack.

And just like that she's on her way.

PART III

The Healing Years

Dear Reader,

The older I've become, the more I have realized that we cannot go forward—evolve—if we don't know or recognize where we have been. While I've always attempted to understand and navigate the many challenges I've faced in my life, with varying degrees of success, it wasn't until this year that I truly made a concerted and dedicated effort to honestly assess my journey in hopes of achieving the inner peace that I felt still eluded me; that inner peace that would allow me to "know the place for the first time" as I arrive at the end of my exploring. I had to look at myself objectively—from another person's perspective, as best I could— and discovered that I am fearless.

But my fearlessness was not easily attained.

Breaking patterns related to generational curses and identity involves a deep understanding of family dynamics, and intentional change. There is no structured approach. What I do know is that I have had to acknowledge and accept that these patterns exist without assigning blame, and recognizing how they have influenced my behavior and identity was vital for my relationships moving forward.

Journaling has given me the opportunity to explore all my personal experiences and their connection to these generational patterns. As I continue to uncover beliefs and behaviors that have been inherited across all families and how they have impacted my life, I began to replace negative habits with positive ones and consistently reinforce change.

Turning fifty this year finally forced me to reflect and reassess these relationships—how they have molded me, challenged me, and enlightened me. Emotional abandonment from my mother, while being left to navigate my fears and struggles without the support I desperately needed from her was instrumental in my healing. And then, thanks to Tristen, narcissistic relationships, I discovered, have been my greatest hurdle besides grief.

This personal project turned into a life review that uncovered a pattern of unhealthy relationships. Whether unsupportive, toxic, or simply unfulfilling, it was clear that I had set myself aside to make these relationships work or attempt to manage them, that I had learned to be what others needed me to be, losing sight of my own needs in the process; and that I compromised my safety and well-being to keep the peace.

This life review became a powerful catalyst for personal change, an opportunity for me to see and celebrate my bravery over the years and make adjustments in my life that would work to heal and promote my well-being. Redefining my identity and creating a vision of the person I want to be, not the person I had to be became powerful in my narrative while working toward my independence of family patterns, my own or others.

As I sit at my desk, looking out the beveled glass window at the ruby throated hummingbirds zip and zoom by, I realize that some of the actions I see are being made in the defense of their nest—nature's own theater on the art of survival. This vision reminds me of watching the robins in our backyard as a little girl. In my youthful mind, I thought it was playfulness. Whether these sightings illustrate play or instincts of survival, they are displays of social interaction—much like the ones humans engage in. There have been countless times I have witnessed this same buzzing behavior in my own life—besieged by a cacophony of conduct that I struggled to understand, aggressive interactions destabilizing my footing.

I needed to heal that eleven-year-old girl who desperately needed to feel love and make sense of loss. I had to make space in my life to hear her again and give her the answers she asked for, so long ago.

I have never had an issue finding my voice. The problem was when I asserted myself and set boundaries, my efforts were not supported. I realized that standing up to a narcissist isn't an easy feat. It's safer to look away, downplay what is occurring, and hope difficult moments fizzle out. Safer until the toxicity catches up with you. Longing for someone to not only protect me but have a partnership with to pass on positive patterns together. My mother and father were my first role models but there were lessons to be learned to empower the next generation.

In time, I finally realized that I could only do what was right for me. I could no longer ignore the injustices swirling around me. This has not been an easy journey, as it requires confronting deeply engrained anger toward men who lead with hubris or are wounded themselves. They lead with an exaggerated façade hiding the deep fear and insecurity they have within themselves. I could no longer allow that bravado and bullying to impact my life. This decision was a crucial step in reclaiming my self-value and worth. It was the step I needed to put my mental health first finally.

Together with the frustration with women in my life who did not provide emotional support, care and guidance and did not put the needs of their children first and center. To me, a mother is multifaceted and plays an essential role in the lives of her children and community. I am learning the definition of a mother can be deeply personal, but I do know what type of mother figure I want to be for my children.

Life is short. Time is fast. No replays and no rewinds. I have found my way forward, and I hope you find yours, too.

love, me

June 1992 to September 1998
Eighteen to Twenty-Four Years Old

Dear Dad,

Grandpa Jim has a lot of influential friends in the community from his years of being an accountant. One of them is Craig Dill, who happens to be the divorce attorney helping Mom. She should be thrilled her dad is alive, let alone present to support her during tough times.

Aside from being Mom's voice at Mr. Dill's office, my job is finding and making copies of important financial documents for Mom and the attorney. A mission I took seriously. Being present with Mom and her lawyer felt empowering. I enjoy making Martin squirm, even if he does not know it yet.

Is that wrong? I don't think it is, considering all the meanness he and his family have put me, Mom, and Shiloh through. Each of his multiple personalities is officially losing control…. well, over me, at least.

I was thinking the other day about a conversation I had with Jared's mother, Marla. We talked about her mom, who is losing her memory, and she spoke about being a caretaker. I had never really heard of that word before. We also discussed my situation and how I feel like I am handling it all at an age that is not normal.

I told her I was angrier about not being seen and heard from people, especially Mom.

Marla is a lovely lady with a genuine smile, twinkling eyes, and a huge heart. I wish you could meet her.

Nobody has ever asked me if I felt understood. I didn't know how to react or respond when Marla did. I didn't say Jared was irritating me. I just said I felt different, but that applies to everything.

I told her those closest to me had never seen or heard me, let alone given me respect. I longed to be understood.

There in front of me was a compassionate woman. Not my mother, but a mother to three children of her own, taking the time to give me admiration and love. A feeling I hadn't felt since you were alive.

I wish she could give Mom a few lessons on loving. I continue to question my understanding of my own mother. But I know, she is my mother and all I really want from her is more safeguarding. I feel as if I have been standing alone in a storm with no shelter, vulnerable to every emotional gust since you died. I like thunderstorms, but not this much.

love, me

Dear Dad,

After we moved out of Spencer Road, we found a place in Saginaw—a small, three-level house with two bedrooms, a bathroom, and a large loft. There are striped scalloped awnings over the front windows that remind me of a café. It has a wooden swing on the porch. Mom uses the basement to cut hair, but she also works at some salons in town.

Mom started dating other Dorky Dudes and would stay out late, leaving me to watch over Shiloh and Brinley Jo. I'm almost nineteen and tired of doing this, let alone trying to figure out my own life. Most of my friends have gone away to college. I am still playing house, it's getting old—when do I get to be free from responsibilities that belong to adults?

You will not be happy to hear that Mom is dating the Demon Dude again. Can you believe it? What in the hell is wrong with her? I just cannot take the senselessness of it all anymore.

Plus, Jared keeps making me angrier, and I have started lying to him about where I go and what I do. He is too jealous, Dad. He is going two hours away to attend college on a golf scholarship, which may give me some space.

I was trying to decide if it would be best to move out of Mom's and live independently. After one night of her coming home at three a.m., I will spare you the details, but I did ask her what she thought being a mom involved. Her answer appalled me and gave me the motivation I needed.

"To take you to church, provide a roof over your head, and food to eat." Enough said. I packed up, and off I went.

love, me

Dear Dad,

My belongings in that box were not as heavy as all the emotional weight I carry. Moving out on my own at nineteen taught me a lot about myself. I am braver than I think and can survive on ramen noodles. I keep taking a few packages from Mom's cupboard when she isn't home or, if lucky, find them at the grocery store for sale at 12 for $1.

My other favorite meal is cheap Chinese for lunch with coworkers at Hunan Garden. Their pricing is doable. Kung Pao Chicken with white rice, an eggroll, and a drink for $5.99 felt like a lot of money, but I could get two meals out of it. On the weekends, if Jared is in town, I have meals with his family which are helpful and allow me to save money.

Uncle Dane was particular about where I lived. There were a few older homes for rent near the courthouse that had some great charm. They were rundown but had character. Uncle Dane wasn't thrilled about the characters running around some of those neighborhoods. He and Aunt Kay gave me their old table, chairs, pots, and pans to help me start living independently.

I didn't have any money. In addition to sneaking some ramen packages and using a few of Mom's dress clothes (she never knew) for the first few months when I started working at Yeo & Yeo. Grandpa Jim is still a partner. After an intense interview with the executive firm manager, Ron, it was determined I would work five days a week, and they would be flexible with hours based on my college classes. For obvious reasons, I could not go away to school and opted for the local community college. It felt right to be closer to Shiloh and Brinley , plus I did not have money, nor did Mom for me. So, I supported myself.

I also officially moved into Camelot Apartments. It took me twenty minutes to get to Delta Community College, where I'm taking classes, and fifteen minutes to get to Yeo & Yeo, where I work as an assistant office manager. I am beside Sandra and Joni, seasoned senior office administrators who showed me how to handle people in business and cranky client demands. The people working at Yeo & Yeo are my favorite part, even the partners who walk tall in their three-piece suits. Coming home to my mauve carpeting and plaid couch was gratifying. I struggled working forty hours and going to school. My homework suffered, but I kept in the B zone without effort.

I cashed in on the bonds I had received growing up for birthdays and holidays. Uncle Dane helped find me a used car at the police auction. I bought it on my own for $1,000. A silver Dodge Omni hatchback. You would laugh at it. I do, but not when it stalls in the intersection when the lights are green.

I've also been working at Aunt Nancy's store in Frankenmuth on the weekends for extra money. She opened Touch of Brass and Taste of Southwest a year ago. They turned the old school on Main Street into a shopping center called School Haus Square.

Jimmy, who works at the old-time candy store, and I cover customers and look out for each other when we need to dash to the bathroom. He gets way more customers than I do. People like candy more than dream catchers, rain sticks, or pieces of brass in the shape of a duck.

I always bring my lunch and eat it in the stockroom on the floor, literally a little closet with a microwave and refrigerator. I can peek through the slits in the door if a customer comes in.

It's not much, Dad, but it's better than what my life was when I was living with Mom.

love, me

Dear Dad,

Life keeps feeling unpredictable and unstable.

Safety feels out of reach, yet I continue to push through. Death, divorce, and dictatorship are a trinity I never learned about in parochial school. I want to make you proud, but more so, I want to make myself proud. When I listen to "Eye of the Tiger," while I'm running, the lyrics feel like they were written for me. I don't have a Coach Mickey in my corner like Rocky, so I am learning to be my coach.

The world around me is continuing to crumble, but I can control how I think and react, which isn't easy. It's sad when I think about how no one ever has tried to understand my confusion.

I am learning to master my emotions in a way only I could access. I started to pretend Grandma Rosie was here with me and giving me advice on what to do, how to respond and act toward Mom and the many others in my life.

I remember Vicar Barber saying, "Forgive and forget, and don't focus on the past."

For years, I lived a double life within myself—a dual personality of what I felt internally and would show externally. The story of my childhood felt too complicated to capture on paper, but heck, maybe I should put the puzzle pieces together?

Maybe I'm trying to put it behind me, but I seem to have trouble tricking my mind lately.

I guess I will keep running.

love, me

Dear Dad,

I was struggling with my school schedule and keeping a job. After almost eighteen months, I decided to leave both. I transferred to a four-year state university and focus on finishing my degree. After completing my undergraduate classes and obtaining an associate's degree from Delta Community College, the best decision was to keep working toward a marketing degree.

At Yeo & Yeo, I was fortunate to shadow and support Barb, their marketing director, manage aspects of promotion and awareness of the account firm's business strategies. I enjoyed learning her process and helped with a few campaigns.

I got a part-time job at a place called the Morning Emporium. It's a couple of miles from my apartment and is a gathering spot for a lot of people. It's more than just serving up great pastries and coffee. I have been meeting so many people within the community, and I know them all by name, along with their drinks.

The homework load from Saginaw Valley State University (SVSU) is intense. I could sit in the cozy coffee shop and do assignments.

After six months, I started working with the Morley Family. Morley Companies is a corporation that services Fortune 500 clients through its travel agency, incentive, and telecommunication departments. Their history is crazy cool. Initially, it was founded in 1863 as a hardware store, and to date is among the oldest surviving companies in the United States. Mrs. Furlo was a regular at the Morning Emporium. Every morning, she ordered a cream cheese pastry warmed with a medium Earl Grey tea latte.

After several conversations, she insisted I speak to her husband, Louis J. Furlo, Sr., at Morley. When I did, I told him I was focused on my schooling and would only be able to accept an internship to get experience in marketing. He smiled and offered me a salaried position onsite despite what I'd told him.

Dad, if only you were there. I held my composure but wanted to scream and jump for joy. Mr. Furlo's secretary, Debby, came to the door and welcomed me to the family. I first started in the tele-communications department as a supervisor for programs.

A few months later, I interviewed for an account executive position in the Incentive Division, which provided travel incentive programs to some of the nation's largest corporations. I learned to be adaptable and reestablish myself from a struggling college student to a young professional having to develop client/supplier contracts, create budgets and proposals, submit RFPs, secure meeting space, and make site visits with clients to five-star hotels.

Things are definitely looking up for me, Dad.

love, me

Dear Dad,

I have been traveling a lot and working long hours. The various cities I have visited are all new to me. My favorites were Washington, D.C. and New York. The hotels are really nice. The people at the hotels have been friendly, and my coworkers and trip directors who help run the programs have been kind, considering I am young compared to many of those around me.

Being responsible for coordinating and leading incentive and motivational events for big companies not only taught me about being highly detailed orientated but also learning to adapt in how I communicate with customers depending on who they are and what company they represent.

Jared proposed while we were in Toronto over my birthday weekend, and I wasn't excited. This should have been an indicator, but I had learned a long time ago how to manage my feelings and relationships in a way that worked for me. It's probably a protective lining that was unconsciously put in place after dealing with Mom and all the drama.

Jared didn't know that I had been seeing other people, which is not something I'm proud of, but I know we aren't suitable for each other. I was meeting polished professional people who exuded confidence and a different type of charisma, a maturity that did not drip with envy and control of my every action.

I am spinning. I feel trapped. I don't feel enthusiasm or eagerness to spend the rest of my life with this guy but fear. There have been plenty of times I wish you were here, Dad, but this is one of those holy-shit-what-did-I-get-myself into moments. Jared and his family kept me sane for all those years, but I don't think I want to spend the rest of my life with him.

I know what I need to do, but letting people down is not one of my strong suits.

I wish you and I could talk things over.

love, me

Dear Dad,

You will never believe what I did! Or couldn't do… I couldn't talk at the bridal shower two nights ago. I had an out-of-body experience, like I knew getting married was wrong. During the gift-giving, I could only focus on Mara, my Morley coworker. Her motherly presence motivated me to get through the last hour. I was flush and red, panicked, and pissed.

After the shower, I called Jared to let him know I was going to have drinks with my friends.

I didn't have to report to him, Dad. It was the right thing to do.

Well, he went ballistic. He drove to my townhouse and waited for me to get home. I cannot begin to tell you how pissed off I was, Dad. Telling my "fiancé" how I just had a bridal shower for our wedding and wanted to grab a drink with my coworkers, all women after, to celebrate the occasion, and he was flipping out.

That was the final straw for me. I told him we are done. I do not want to get married. This was wrong for both of us. He was not thrilled.

Of course, I was angry at him, but I knew marrying him was wrong the moment he proposed. We were only four months away from the wedding day. Coordinating all the details was easy. Undoing them and returning all the bridal shower gifts wasn't going to be that easy.

So instead, I hopped on a plane to NYC for a program I was putting on for a client. This weeklong program came at the most convenient time. I was immersed in work but had a blast when free time presented itself. I got to walk down Times Square with some coworkers.

What an experience, Dad.

You would have loved it. Brightly lit digital billboards everywhere. I walked next to some young guy with a boa constrictor draped around his neck. Lynda told me not to look up at the buildings because that is what tourists do. Seeing those things made me want to do more. There was a fire lit inside me that had never been there before. Or maybe it had and I'd just ignored it.

Upon my return, I had a wedding to attend. Amy Sage was one year older than me. Do you remember her? She lived over by the pond where Grandma and I would ice skate. Thinking about Grandma makes me miss her. I try to talk to her once every week.

Jared was scheduled to come with me to Amy's wedding reception. I had left New York and my program early to make the party, and he and I had not talked the entire time I was away. You can imagine how the night ended, in a fight. He said I was making a big mistake and maybe I was, but it felt right.

Even though I had no idea what the future would hold for me and how many people I was upsetting.

I couldn't bring myself to cut him out of my life though. I loved his family. I understood the tradeoff, but the price of not having that sense of security they brought was greater than dealing with this guy, who was too protective and not for me.

I hope that's not a mistake.

love, me

Dear Dad,

I have been home for less than a week. Jared sent me roses at work. I keep my distance from him. Jared's mom and his sister-in-law, Michelle, have called me to ask why I cancelled the wedding.

I tell them they don't understand.

Aside from him being highly jealous and wanting to do weird things in the bedroom. I will spare you the details. I don't like it, though. I still have that time when I overheard Mom with Martin which is probably worthy of a therapy session.

My boss told me I was going to Florida in two days for a familiarization trip, also known as a FAM program. I was fortunate to be chosen to go alongside Susie and Brian, Susie's boss. They have taken me under their wing and taught me much.

These FAM trips allow planners like me to experience the sites for meeting space and excursions for consideration for upcoming events I may book. Hilton and American Airlines invited their top clients to travel to their Disney property in Orlando in June. I am so excited.

The only thing weighing me down is that I need to determine what to do about Jared and these wedding plans I have yet to cancel.

love, me

Dear Dad,

You will never believe what happened at this gathering in Florida.

It was pure fate how we met, Dad—in the most peculiar place, doing the quirkiest thing. I am not sure if it was his playful cinnamon-colored eyes that gazed at me across the aluminum worktop in the oversized commercial kitchen, but it felt like his stare went deep into my soul.

We had both happened to be in the hotel kitchen for an immersive culinary experience for the conference. We learned new cooking techniques and recipes for making a dessert but also experienced the professional environment of the hotel kitchen.

Tim took this opportunity to interact with the chef, the cuisine, and me. His contagious smile spread to my corner of the table. From that moment on, no one else existed at lunch. I saw him later at an evening reception and he asked me if I was going to the bar after dinner. I coyly stated, "If you are going, then I may too."

Tim is the Assistant Director of Sales for the San Diego Hilton. We are attended the same corporate event for our respective companies. I had been to Disney with Mom and Shiloh shortly after you died. Mom thought visiting Grandma and taking us to theme parks would be good. I never liked crowds and lines, this time hit different.

I laughed when Tim told me, "Your finger may be engaged, but your heart is not."

You would like him, Dad. I have no doubt. His sense of humor is similar to yours.

His smile appeared warm and genuine as he later asked me about my chances of coming to California in less than two weeks. I have two weeks of honeymoon vacation I will not be using, so why not?

Officially ending my relationship with Jared felt rebellious. I should have done it sooner, but no matter what, it was a tough, awkward, and uncomfortable way to end our time together.

Tim was the catalyst.

Everything sped up, and this was the change I had wanted, but had been avoiding all those years.

I have no remorse or regret for ending that chapter in my life with Jared and his family, even though it was hard.

Now, here I go—into unchartered waters without that life preserver.

love, me

Dear Dad,

I decided to move to California on Mom's birthday, September 13.

Tim asked if he could fly to Michigan to meet Mom and Shiloh and then drive back to California with me. Who does that, Dad? This guy is wooing me. No one has ever made me feel like Tim does.

Moving away from Michigan helped me gain some clarity on things. Listening to my instincts has always boded me well. Moving on has been a survival tactic that I have mastered.

Well, maybe not mastered, but honed.

I feel confident this move to California will jumpstart a new life, a new feeling of family, connection, and community of people to strengthen my emotional well-being and help me move past my pain.

love, me

Dear Dad,

Even though I rented a house in Del Mar, I was basically living with Tim because he would often call and ask me to come over after work. One particular night, he was adamant that I change my work clothes into something swankier. We were going to a restaurant at the posh Rancho Valencia Resort and Spa, a lovely hotel tucked away on endless acres of lush gardens and olive groves.

I wasn't surprised. Tim does these random things. I had just returned from a conference in Montreal and Quebec, so he wanted to have a nice romantic dinner since I'd been gone for Valentine's Day.

Tim appeared jumpy as we walked into the Mediterranean château. We walked past the bubbling fountain and drank a glass of wine in the Pony Room. The hostess walked us back through the inviting courtyard with overgrown fuchsia bougainvillea creeping out from pots to a table for two directly in front of a fireplace with an open flame.

Dad, you can guess what happened next. I honestly had no clue.

Tim got down on one knee and proposed. I do not remember what he said or how he said it... all I recall is saying, "Are you for real?"

He said, "The ring is not real. I borrowed it. You get to pick out what you want!"

I laughed out loud because this was a typical thing for him to do. I can't believe it! I'm engaged!

love, me

Dear Dad,

Today, on August 1, 1998, Tim gave my heart a home.

The wedding was nothing short of spectacular.

We got married at the Four Seasons Aviara in Carlsbad, California. With my background in meeting planning and Tim's in hotels, we were bound to have a hell of an event. His side contributed a substantial amount of money to the festivities, which made Mom feel her donation to the day was puny based on the setting and all the extras. We, of course, never talked about it.

I was sad that Grandma Hogan wasn't in attendance, but I know crazy crowds and airplanes are not her thing. She was deeply missed, but my feelings for her never wane, Dad. Similar to how I feel about you.

All my memories and moments of our time together keep the bond alive in my heart and mind, which brings comfort and a sense of connection even though you are not here with me today. Our love transcends physical presence. You still influence me. This is a feeling I will forever hold onto.

Tim's dad walked me down the aisle, which was the right decision. I think I wanted him to play a father role for me, or maybe because I couldn't decide between Grandpa Jim and Uncle Dane.

At times throughout the day, it felt uncomfortable being with Mom and seeing her in my new life. I always wanted more from her, but never asked for her to give me more. We've never talked about feelings in the past. Why start on my wedding day?

I want to feel closer to Mom, but something prevents it. I had to deal with Shiloh and her shenanigans too. She's acting selfish and was supposed to be with me in the bridal suite the night before my wedding instead of partying with Tim's friends. I get she is only sixteen, at that age we tend to be self-centered, but I get tired of no one thinking of how I feel. At sixteen, I had to think of others. I couldn't be selfish even when I wanted to. I really get tired of always having to be responsible.

I could tell by the way Shiloh was acting together with Mom and her boyfriend, Dick, that Mom still isn't taking care of her own shit. I always feel like I didn't do something right or need to babysit their feelings. It's a consistent feeling, even on my wedding day. Here I am, trying to make my mother feel whole, but not myself. And trying to make sure my little sister is not in the hotel room smoking pot and drinking on my wedding night.

Dick seems to be a nice, solid guy even though he was friends with Mom's ex-husband. I don't know him that well. He and I had a brief chat before I moved to California. Dick was supportive and knew my decision was made but gave me good stepdad vibes. I like to assume Mom was reserved because she and Dick did not know many people at the wedding. On my side, less than a handful of family members showed up.

Aunt Kay and Uncle Dane didn't attend. Mom told me their flight back from Hawaii stopped in Los Angeles the day before we were to get married. I guess they must have been pretty mad that Uncle Dane wasn't going to walk me down the aisle.

I wonder what you would think of their behavior. I understand their hurt feelings, but they should also respect my choices. Sometimes, I think they expect certain things since they helped me out during those hard times, and you and Uncle Dane were close like brothers. But to me, being a family is about loving and helping each other unconditionally. Am I wrong?

love, me

Dear Dad,

Tim and I are back from our honeymoon.

I cannot even begin to convey the memorable time we had together.

We saw some spectacular places and met wonderful people, and the food was ridiculously delicious. I ate more tasty cheese and flaky croissants in Paris than a body should.

The cheese carts rolling around after dinner at several restaurants were a mouse's dream.

My favorite stop in Giverny was visiting Monet's Gardens, the home and grounds of the famous French impressionist painter Claude Monet.

He had a way of composing and cultivating what he saw and bringing it to life in his famous paintings.

Seeing his inspiration live was priceless.

You would have appreciated the landscaping and layout, but not his pink house.

We then meandered over to Zurich, Switzerland.

Every restaurant served fondue, a hot pot of melting cheese and wine. I never got the hang of using the long-stemmed forks to dip the bread and vegetables in. I used my fingers, and Tim didn't seem to mind.

The landscape is very different in Switzerland.

We trained into Italy, the next and last country we visited.

You would truly appreciate the serenity of the outdoors.

Our last stops were Lake Como, Florence, and Venice.

I don't even know which one I liked more.

Venice is not only a major Italian port, Dad, but a pretty picturesque city, with water taxis taking you to and from your hotels and all the winding canals and beautiful bridges. After our architecture tour, we ate anchovy pizza for lunch in the famous piazza.

You would have liked people-watching and probably would have liked the pizza since you always ate those smoked oysters in a can on top of potato chips. Tim and I both agreed to pick them off.

We are a good fit, Dad. He makes me smile and knows how to have a good time. He doesn't seem to take life too seriously, which I greatly appreciate and need.

I have been feeling sick to my stomach lately, which I thought was from all the wine and rich foods I have been consuming. But Tim ordered chicken on the plane back to the U.S. and it smelled like sour milk.

He disagreed, so I took a pregnancy test after we got home.

Actually, I took three of them.

Guess what...

love, me

Dear Dad,

I've immersed myself in Tim's family. I was searching for that father figure, not to replace you, but to feel supported. I know you would have wanted this for me, too. Calling my father-in-law a father figure sounds incredibly wrong, but I think I have spent most of my life searching for the type of role model who emits the same qualities I admired and respected about you.

I had high hopes of building a genuine relationship and connection with my father-in-law.

Tim and I came into this marriage wanting the same thing—a partnership—while creating a happy, lasting, and fulfilling family environment, which is something neither of us had. Well, I felt I had it for the first few years. Then Tim and his father started working together, and our lives began to interweave. The more time spent together meant more nuances to see.

My father-in-law was involved with financial planning and had done well for himself, affording the family certain luxuries. They lived in Los Angeles and had a nice home and drove nice cars but did not seem flashy.

However, how they spend their money differs significantly from how we did. My father-in-law appears to be a workaholic.

His identity is money management, reading the papers and any other research material his wife prints out and places in front of him. He liked to only talk about things that interested him. This was very different than Grandpa Jim and Grampie, and your dad never really talked to anyone.

Being part of Tim's family gave me an interesting insight. What I am learning, Dad, is that all families are dysfunctional and messy.

Their family dynamic continues to intrigue me. I never really thought about it early on.

But as time passes, we are forced to look at things differently.

Tim's stepmother has been in the picture since he was four years old, but their relationship seems to be built on an expectation for reciprocation. Initially, it seemed like my step-mother-in-law really liked me, and I felt love-bombed, in a good way. There was plenty of wedding talk and planning. She even had her seamstress custom-make the bridesmaids' gowns and jeweler design the necklaces. I remember feeling like this with Aunt Kay—our relationship was conditional based on what she gave me and what I did for her in return. I remember thinking when Aunt Kay and Uncle Dane had my high school graduation party at their house, they made a big deal about it and held it over my head and against Mom, which I thought was strange. Family should do those things, right? We should give to each other without the expectation of receiving something in return, like material objects or conditions to reciprocate. Transactional behaviors don't equal love.

I hope I am wrong, but honestly, Dad, I notice she just does whatever my father-in-law wants. Maybe I am feeling some similarities with Mom?

Tim's mom is in his life, together with her third husband, but lives thirty minutes outside Los Angeles. Tim doesn't seem too close with his mom. When I first met her, I couldn't believe how much Tim looked like her. She was the female version of my husband but with hair. She was a very pleasant woman, and I genuinely felt she cared.

What is concerning is I have seen a few of Martin's traits with my father-in-law such as mood swings and a sort of emotional numbness. He only talks when you ask him questions, and only lights up when he's talking about topics he likes. He likes to act like he is more intelligent and better than everyone else and expects people to cater to his needs.

I'm thankful you were never like that. I don't think it's a behavior you grow into; you are either a kind human or you are not. I'm not going to say anything to Tim, at least not yet, but I am concerned.

I can see how my father-in-law and his wife didn't stay married. She is feisty and would probably have told my father-in-law to kick rocks. When she hosted a wedding shower for me, she was very inclusive and asked me what I preferred.

However, I've noticed she can also be very devious and has her own conniving ways. For example, she invited us several times to go to Yosemite and I told her no each time. We aren't much for hiking, however, at Christmas she gave us hotel vouchers to go there. There are other things that I don't want to get into, but this is ongoing.

I had to create a boundary. She ended up taking Tim to therapy. While there, he told her she had the wrong person there, and she invites me next visit sans Tim. I, of course, went with my list of her many shenanigans and tell the therapist as we speak of all her behaviors. That was the last time I went to therapy with her.

In short, Tim again never stood up for me or himself due to his own trauma as a kid—but it caused a rift for us as I was tired of being his armor with his parents.

In the end things settled down, but he never found his voice.

I can relate to that. Look at my relationship with Mom. That is far from ideal.

Tim said he remembers them fighting a lot. I guess you and Mom were not that different in the marriage club. We both know what it feels like to have a miserable relationship with our families and that lack of love from those closest to us.

So maybe Tim is struggling with parental love, too. I don't know and am not sure how to approach the matter.

We have so many other distractions. My pregnancy has been bumpy, but I know it will be beautiful in the end, Dad. You would laugh if you could see me. My body does not like being pregnant. Nonstop nausea is not for the faint of heart. The doctor told me to consume less sodium and to cut out the highly processed comfort foods I like so much.

The good news is that I will be giving birth soon. I look forward to creating a happy and healthy environment for our children, that same feeling you and I had.

love, me

May 1999-April 2004
Twenty-five to Thirty Years Old

Dear Dad,

The doctor had very pregnant me on bedrest at thirty-one weeks. This same attentive doctor told me to lessen my cottage cheese intake, too, as my sodium numbers were skyrocketing. It may have been all the crappy food I was intaking to forgo the nausea. I know you will keep my secrets safe, Dad. She told me that having one cup of cottage cheese is like a handful of potato chips. Who knew? I would rather have had the chips.

I learned a few fun facts and will share them with you.

When the doctor told Tim and me when a woman's cervix is fifty percent effaced, it's halfway to becoming short and thin enough to allow the baby to pass through the uterus and into the vagina—which meant nothing to me at that point. Sometimes, doctors assume you know what they are saying and forget we are not trained in this medical jargon. I wonder if you had this same experience with all the cancer talk you had to absorb during your two-year confrontation with cancer, and I can only imagine an assortment of foreign medical vocabulary.

What we were told is most effacement usually happens during the first stage of labor, so they wanted to slow Mr. Cole Thomas from coming out. I was already dilated to one centimeter and had fifty percent effacement in the thirty-first week, which they needed to slow to keep Cole from coming, which meant I had to lie flat unless I had to get up to go to the bathroom and shower. I was shocked. I was being told not to move.

Oh, Dad, the fact I was bedridden or rather "couch prison" was awful. Thank goodness for our comfortable and oversized couch. I did manage to work from home but was clamoring to get up and go anywhere besides two rooms (bathroom and bedroom) in the house.

The fact that Tim had to make dinner and perform duties was a riot.

His two executed meals were egg salad sandwiches on white bread and pasta. The biggest failure with the first meal was putting sweet relish in the mix, which is gross. Nobody in our family likes sweet relish. But I appreciated his efforts. Besides Chinese takeout, his second meal was bowtie pasta with chunks of chicken swimming in cream of mushroom soup. Did that ever bring back memories? He cares, and I am grateful for that, Dad, even though his culinary skills need improvement.

Did you ever make dinner for Mom or me? I remember you making me a big bowl of Schwan vanilla ice cream every night but nothing else.

As you know, I thrive on being active. I don't like television. Unless it is educational or keeps me interested, TV is just not my thing.

Having to relax forces every cell in my body to chill, which they and I are not used to; of course, I did my best to follow instructions but failed frequently. By nature, I guess I am an antsy person. Hence, laying down and not being able to sit was also a struggle; it felt like forever, but they let me off bedrest.

The day after I was released from couch prison, my water broke, which brings you up to date with what's happening in real time.

I had been slowly taking on fewer programs at work, and I changed jobs before Cole arrived. Balboa Meetings and Motivation was a great company, and the commute was closer to home. Driving to downtown San Diego and working late hours got to be draining. Tim liked having me home, too, and I enjoyed living a more relaxed lifestyle, something I was not accustomed to.

love, me

Dear Dad,

Well, here I am, officially a mom!

Cole Thomas Cohen was born in May 1999. My whole world turned upside down when I held him.

His hair is cinnamon like yours, with big brown eyes, and he has a sweet, calm character. He barely cries and loves to lay cuddled up on my chest. There is nothing more heartwarming and moving than this feeling, Dad. Absolutely nothing.

I remember seeing Shiloh's footprints on your arm the day she was born. You were beaming. I had never seen you smile so big. I can relate now.

I am thankful for the nurse. She was like a mother to me.

Delivery was easy, and for some reason, this little guy wanted to get here and hang with me.

Cole is healing a side of me that I never knew I needed to be healed. Trite, I think, but true.

Having this beautiful boy has brought light to the sadness I had hidden deep down. I am fortunate to have found love around me, both with my son and husband.

love, me

Dear Dad,

Mom arrived a few days ago to meet her grandson. Watching her hold Cole has softened my scorn for her. I need to remind myself she did her best considering all the circumstances thrown her way. I still do not agree with some of the choices she made. I get that we all do things differently. But it doesn't take away some of the pain I still feel.

My biggest issue is how she didn't choose her children first. Especially as a mom now, there is something protective that takes over. I would never allow anything to compromise my child. I want to safeguard him and give him the harmony I never had.

Despite my lingering resentment, I have enjoyed spending time with Mom. We've been going to lunch and taking Cole on walks while Tim is at work. Last night, he met Mom and me for dinner at a nautical-themed restaurant. Mom ordered their infamous fish tacos and a margarita.

My apologies for not writing as often as I used to, but please know that I think of you all the time. I feel hectic and harried most days, and the last thing I want to do is sit down to write. I can't do it all, even though I try.

love, me

Dear Dad,

My job has been hectic. I've been traveling and meeting with clients, which my boss has praised me for. I felt seen, which felt good. I am proud of myself and know I can do much more, but truth be told, I am unsure how long I can sustain this workload and travel.

I like being home with Cole, and Tim is pushing me to "retire early," as he called it. I have dreamed of having a family, being a mom, and creating what I lost after you died. The struggle is really hard, Dad.

I'm considering stepping away from the corporate world but am stressed about not having my own source of income. I don't want to be dependent on someone, not even my husband. I have been in survival mode for so long. I know Tim loves me, but I still feel a sense of self-protection. I'm not sure if it is right to feel this way. We have talked about it, and Tim understands my sensitivity but keeps reminding me that I can always make money, but I can never get these precious times back with my sweet son.

I was blessed to grow up with you for a short time.

Respectable parenting requires an unapologetic decision to raise a child, and I know I am ready and able. You showed me total love and devotion and helped me to see my value early on. I will honor this and thread all my earliest memories and simple acts you showed me into his life. I promise.

love, me

Dear Dad,

Out of respect for Mom and my upbringing, I decided to fly back to Michigan and have Cole baptized. As his mother, whatever he ends up choosing religiously, I don't want to be responsible for any original sin on his sweet soul.

It was nice being back home for a short visit and seeing everyone. I chose Shiloh to be his godparent, even though she's only eighteen. I trust she could make good decisions on his behalf, with Mom's help, if something happened to me.

Not many can photograph five generations at the front of the baptismal foundation. I was later told what a rare occurrence that moment was. I never really thought about it until Tim pointed out how priceless it was to have Grampie, Grandpa Jim, and Mom with us that day. Despite everything, I am feeling very lucky these days.

love, me

Dear Dad,

I decided to leave my job and be a full-time mom.

I have never been without work, now that I think about it. After you died, Aunt Kay had me cut felt pads for the foot patients after surgery for Dr. Simpson. I then went with her several times and helped answer the phones when I was in eighth grade. I then worked at McDonald's after I hurt my knee and couldn't play sports in high school. The people were so much fun. One of the managers, named Tabby, became a very dear friend.

Even at thirty-two, Tabby and I connected more than anyone else. My favorite memory with her was having Chinese food and drinking Boones Farm Strawberry wine at her place. I also hung out with Chris, another manager. He took me on his motorcycle several times.

I never told Mom that.

I guess I lived a double life, Dad. I became very good at masking my emotions. The "mask" I would wear changed according to the scenario. I learned to hide my emotions and way of being for the sake of others and, more often, because no one cared or asked. All those feelings fell behind a façade to protect myself.

Maybe, at times, we all force ourselves to fit in. Being adaptable is different than conforming. I don't like the feeling of adhering to anyone's expectations, and that's for sure. I'm highly adaptable and have a natural ability to adjust to changing circumstances.

Spending time with my husband and new son while falling into a routine of marriage and motherhood has been bittersweet. I'm fortunate that, financially, we can make this decision. I am pinching myself.

love, me

Dear Dad,

Grandma Rosie came to California for a visit! Can you believe it?

Having her here was nothing short of amazing. We played lots of gin, rummy, and euchre. On the second day, we ate at one of my favorite local restaurants. Grandma had fried calamari for the first time.

She wasn't impressed.

She did like all the different floral varieties here in California. Her favorite plant is the bird-of-paradise. She laughed that there was not a lot of open space and yards here and little grass to grow and mow. She held Cole endlessly, and it made me feel all those emotions I had back when I was eleven, and she was my rock when you died.

It all felt surreal, Dad. Seeing Grandma here and sharing this time with her is something I will forever cherish. Sometimes, you never realize how much someone means to you until you see them after such a long time. When I lived at Martin's, we barely saw each other. That continued when I was traveling, working, and going to university but we did talk more on the phone as I got older. I would always call her for recipes, but they never turned out like hers.

I love that wonderful woman so much, Dad. I am sure you did, too. There are no words to describe how it felt to see Grandma hold Cole and read him bedtime stories. I wonder if Grandma read to you when you were little. She fostered a lifelong love of reading for me. Her storytelling will always have a special place in my soul. It provided a safe place to listen, learn, and laugh. The bond we created through story time is something no one could replace.

In college, one of my professors talked about how books are transformative—they can take us to faraway places, open our hearts and minds, teach us to see each other and bring us together.

Your sister bought Cole a book, which is sweet, too.

I'm getting much more sentimental than I used to be. Maybe it's the hormones!

Aunt Cathleen and Cousin Kate were instrumental in getting Grandma here. We had the best time together. Grandma stayed back to watch Cole while the rest of us went to Tijuana, Mexico. Living close to the border here in San Diego allows us to be in another country in less than forty five minutes.

Aside from walking up and down *Avenida Revolucion*, which is a famous street ten minutes from the border crossing where you can shop for tons of trinkets and, of course, tequila. Tim claims that a hot dog wrapped in bacon, sold by one of the vendors late at night, cures any potential hangover.

I didn't want Grandma to go, so I begged her to stay. She said, "Oh no, the walleye here are not as good as back home." I am missing the Midwest more than I thought. It is probably the familiarity and, of course, having family around.

Selfishly, watching Grandma again, now that I am older and having moved away, I sense how honest, proud, yet modest she is and not afraid to get her hands dirty. I like that I have those same traits. I often tell her that I am her favorite grandchild. She denies it, but her blue eyes twinkle and that rascal smile appears.

I have been thinking a lot about family dynamics. Tim's family has been hospitable to me, but there is still a disconnect. They don't feel as authentic. I guess everyone has a different version of family. Perhaps I have too high of an expectation of them, Dad.

Watching their interactions with each other is fascinating. Of course, I compare them to the patterns of interactions I was raised with and around. But now, with Cole and being a mother beginning to build my family system, I want to create a loving and supportive setting where we respect and see each other for who we are but also communicate openly, which was a big missing piece of my childhood that I longed for.

Maybe all families are messy. Maybe ours will be, too, but I promise you one thing: Cole will never feel abandoned like I did.

love, me

Dear Dad,

So much is changing.

Once again.

Tim is in the process of starting a new work venture and we've realized that this house is no longer going to work for us. Packing up to move while pregnant and being a bit emotional is not for the faint of heart. Yeppers, I am having another little one!

Cole is only seven months old, so this was definitely a surprise.

There are so many changes each time I write to you, and I can hardly keep them straight, let alone share them. I try to give you bullet points and not bore you with all the dull but delightful details.

I am still surprised myself. I am due in October.

Tim and I have only been married less than two years and after these first two years of mostly married bliss, I still have to remind him that I don't enjoy socializing as much as he does. He loves to entertain people, but sometimes I think he forgets he is a married man with a baby. I am not the nagging nor the jealous type, and as I look around and pack up, there are plenty of stories these walls could share.

But now there are different responsibilities, we can't straddle both, and you know my backstory—I always had to be the adult and here I am again, leading the way when he should be telling his friends those days are over.

I am hopeful this move will be a break away from some of his pre-marriage behaviors. My gripe may sound petty, but there have been several of these moments, and I am beginning to sound like Mom now.

Interesting, right?

Mom mentioned your inability to grow up many times but is pretty tight-lipped about your drinking days. I will ask her to share more one of these days. Maybe you and Tim share similar behaviors, or perhaps it's just men in general. I don't know.

Much of this is behavior left over from his college days. Sometimes, I wish I had the opportunity to go away to college, live on campus, and join a sorority. But then, thinking back, I liked living alone and having my own space and solitude. Being around people all the time exhausts me, but it may have made me more tolerable and less fussy.

At this point, we are parents—his partying days are over, and my responsibilities continue differently. Moving away from our social scene and charting a new career course and chapter in our lives will bring maturity and growth. Here we go!

love, me

Dear Dad,

Well, here I am—a mom of another boy!

Cody Jed Cohen was born in September 2000. I never knew my heart could hold the amount of love for two beautiful boys.

Tim has a theory, "It takes a man to make a man," which is ridiculous. But this is another sneak peek into the machismo he displays for a funny joke. I told you the two of you are more alike than not.

I am blessed to have Cody. He has a sweet soul. I can already sense it— my connection to him is powerful. He was just as eager to arrive early as his big brother fifteen months ago was. Thank goodness, I did not have to go on bed rest but did go into labor over one month early. Labor was not nearly as easy as it was the first time.

It felt like I was dying, Dad. It was as if I was hovering over the entire picture of giving birth and could see myself and partake, but I was not there. They took him immediately into neonatal intensive care, as the surfactant in his lungs was not developed yet due to his early arrival. I didn't even know what was taking place. I was out of it until I woke up and asked Tim where my baby was.

My mother-in-law had been watching Cole and brought him to the hospital to see me. He was shuffling around, sneaking cold pancakes off the breakfast tray, and sitting in the corner on a chair. I was emotional seeing him, and he sat on my lap while Tim wheeled us to see his new baby brother in that incubator.

Seeing my newborn hooked up to IVs was distressing. Everything in that controlled environment was keeping him safe and helping to regulate his oxygen levels to support his development. Still, the monitoring was not what a mother wanted to see.

Cole was unfazed and wanted more cold pancakes.

I kept it all together the best I could. Outside, I looked like I was managing it decently, but inside, I was a tangled mess of emotions. All I needed to do was look at my sons, and I would get a second wind.

Leaving the hospital without Cody was tough, but I trusted the doctors and nurses. Science and medicine are sometimes pretty remarkable. I wish they had been able to save you.

There have been plenty of times when things feel too much. I have to mentally repeat to have patience. We live a very chaotic life, and I try to give myself grace and remind myself of my grit.

This is a daily conversation, Dad.

We do have a kidney bean-shaped pool at our new house. Cole likes playing in the pool and in his sandbox.

Cody is still small and attached to my hip, or more accurately tucked in the sling I use to carry him. My parenting paradigm is something I keep living and leaning into. The routine I have shaped is loose but tight. I want Cole and Cody to be adaptable.

Spending my days with two toddlers is a blessing. Each is full, leaving me exhausted and defeated. I tweak the routine based on Tim's schedule and our social calendar. The majority of the time, Tim is gone the entire day and returns in time for dinner.

After dinner, it is family time and Tim will join in the bedtime routine. After baths with rubber duckies floating everywhere, we hang out in Cole's room and read books while cuddling and leaning against two massive stuffed bears. Oso is black, and Lulu is brown.

I like how Tim and I give the boys a sense of safety, confidence, and, most importantly, a predictable environment. I'm so happy we have been able to give them the security that we both were lacking in our childhoods.

love, me

Dear Dad,

At twenty-six, I feel like I'm muddling through, trying to figure out how to be a wife and mom. I hope to not only get through the day but also try to nurture these boys the best way I can.

Every day is an endless activity. I don't have time for anything. My extra moments are none. No complaints, only overtiredness. All the constant motion does not allow much time for thinking and relaxing.

There is a different respect for Mom now—all her behind-the-scenes work. I don't know how involved you were, but I remember her wanting more from you.

I can empathize.

I don't like it here in the "Valley," as the locals call it since it is situated in the San Fernando Valley. Its proximity to L.A. is convenient, but it is far too close for me. I don't fit in here.

There is too much traffic, and people are not as warm as they are back home. I wanted to raise my children in a community like we had, Dad. This lifestyle feels too crowded, fast-paced, and overwhelming. We opted to start in this area because it is where most of Tim's family lives.

When we moved into our appealing ranch one-level home several months before Cody was born, it felt nice being a mile away from his sister's house. His brother lived in Santa Monica, which would be only twenty minutes if traffic played nice. My mother-in-law was now only thirty minutes away. But the massive amount of land just north of Los Angeles was officially purchased in April 2000.

Tim needed to live in Ventura County, where the land is located, for business and political reasons. So, guess what?

We are now moving *yet again*.

This time, it will be farther north, closer to where Tim will spearhead the land's development. He likes the engineering company he has worked with, organized and run by a husband-and-wife team. They live in a bedroom community called Camarillo. We have met with them several times and have explored the area to start this next crazy chapter.

I am thankful for this move, despite how close it was to the other, and I can gladly say I will never be a resident of Los Angeles County again.

love, me

Dear Dad,

When we decided to move closer to the ranch and Camarillo, we had difficulty finding a home. After looking, we found a semi-custom build where they were pouring foundations. The timing was not ideal, and we had to live in an apartment in Camarillo for almost seven months while the construction of the house was complete.

All I can say about the time in this apartment is a blur. I spent much of that time potty training Cole and keeping my wits about me the best I can. Teaching him has been pretty easy. I would give him stickers for a well-done job and loads of positive praise, and he liked the idea of creating a sticker mosaic on the inside lid. Whatever his incentive was, it worked. He was trained by two.

Cody loves to dance and sing from the shows he watches. He's pretty funny. You would laugh at his antics right along with me.

The other day, I walked into the kitchen area. Now, mind you, Dad, it's a minimal space. Still, Cole managed to scamper his way up on the kitchen counter and into a space meant for decorative items and laid straight as a board in this window box. He said he was sunning himself. I couldn't help but laugh.

I constantly think about how you would interact with each of them and how much involvement you would have. I try not to overthink it. I get depressed when I do. I think about you being here more than I should.

At this point, my focus is on keeping the boys safe and healthy, myself sane, and my husband happy despite his workload, let alone working with the custom home builders. I need five of Me's right now. Thanks for understanding my lack of letters to you.

love, me

Dear Dad,

It has been a few years since I've written to you. Life got crazy, and I never made the time.

The boys are now four and five. They attend Carden School in preschool and kindergarten.

Tim continues to be immersed at the ranch as more opportunities materialized over the years. At the beginning, he was solely handling the agricultural development. This has grown and grown, and we now have a dude ranch, a hotel, and a food truck to cater horse events. Honestly, Dad, it's too much and the chaos of our lives is taking a toll.

Tim and I have struggled to work well together recently. He has an "it's my way or the highway" approach to leadership, whereas I'm the opposite. I am receptive to the whole and like to build a collective environment. I step in when I must, but it seems to be more and more. Truly, every role is taking its toll. From managing weddings and catering for filming and dude ranch events, to handling all food prep and shopping, Costco runs included. I am organizing everything, designing hotel interiors and constantly running around like a madwoman all with two little ones in car seats.

In my writing, or lack thereof, I may need to escape or ask for grace in my deficiency of direction in marriage and motherhood. Though all of this is overwhelming, and I sometimes wonder what I've gotten myself into, I push myself to be the best mom possible. My impact is important for the boys and Tim.

I have tried my best to move on with my life, but there is still this urge to have you here. I still miss our shenanigans.

I incorporate some tough love with my boys like you did with me, but always much more affection.

One unexpected turn of events is that Shiloh is now living with me. She told us that her boyfriend was mistreating her. We took her in, and she still hasn't returned to Michigan. Mom went and collected her clothes and stuff from her boyfriend's place. I am not sure this was the best decision I should have made, but I have spent so much of my life protecting her, I don't think I know how to stop.

She lives in a detached, self-contained part of our house that we remodeled for her. This has caused some trouble with Mom and added some stress on me and my marriage and, of course, mothering, now once more again.

I had hoped that I would find the same relationships with Tim's family that I had with Jared's. Jared's family was like a safe haven for me. In Tim's family, however, there is a lack of familial warmth, a bit emotionally detached even among themselves, but hey I can relate unfortunately. But this is not the family dynamic I'd been hoping to have. When I told my father-in-law some sensitive situations that occurred with Martin and Mom and how Jared's family was "like a life preserver" during those times, he had the audacity to call me a user and taker. I really wanted to see him as a father figure since I hadn't had one since you'd died, but that verbal attack took me right back to living in hell.

What is wrong with people, Dad? I am tired of feeling betrayed. I trusted him with my vulnerability and he turned it against me. Chalk it up as another violation of trust—another unexpected attack from someone I hoped would be supportive.

That hurt. His rejection brought back all those issues from my youth and feeling neglected and unwanted. I am in an endless internal battle trying to figure everything out. I crave love, attention, and acceptance. Stabbed in the back again, I am really tired of feeling humiliated for having revealed my deepest thoughts to people.

I really wish you were here to tell my father-in-law what an asshole comment that was. I did, but coming from a woman, doesn't seem to affect this man.

All I can say is there has been no greater adjustment than learning the ropes of adulthood. Being hurled into unrelenting responsibility for two little humans fifteen months apart has been a daunting task. I knew motherhood wouldn't be easy.

But along the way, Dad, I am evolving into a new identity, of which I am unsure what it is besides being a *mother*. I never really

thought about marriage and the work that is involved. I'm struggling to figure out how to handle it all.

It doesn't help that Shiloh is also being a handful. She often
shows me a lack of gratitude and respect for what I am doing
to help her, or maybe it's just her behavior that comes across as
unappreciative. I am not holding grudges, that is not my style but
the constant drama she circulates gets old. She married one of
Tim's friends and her Hawaiian wedding was a debacle. She and
I didn't speak for nearly a year after that, and she wasn't speaking
to Mom either.

I don't know exactly why, but I felt compelled to write her a
letter:

To my sister:

*Today, I sat at the park and watched two young girls
giggle as they climbed onto a merry-go-round. The sound
of their laughter carried me back to our own childhood—
those carefree moments when the world felt lighter and
full of wonder despite Dad's death. I could see us, holding
tightly to the metal bars, laughing as we spun in circles,
daring the dizziness, finding brief moments of stillness
before the world whirled again.*

*A wave of emotion washed over me—both warmth
and then ache. In many ways, it feels like we have never
stopped spinning. Sometimes we spin together. At other
times, we find ourselves on entirely different rides.*

*Our relationship is constantly evolving. From the sim-
plicity of sisterhood to the complexities of marriage and
motherhood, life has taken us in different directions. And*

yet, you are my sister, and there will always be a thread woven through our relationship, colored by the full spectrum of our shared memories, both good and bad.

For that, I am genuinely grateful.

We have had our differences, and I acknowledge they often felt divisive. But I am beginning to see how those very differences have shaped us. As we have grown, we have both struggled to feel fully understood by others. Perhaps that is part of why we retreat at times—why solitude can feel safer than sisterhood.

I recognize my part in us. If my honesty ever felt harsh or if I lacked the empathy you needed, I am sorry. After Dad died, I stepped into a role I did not choose. If I could have simply been your sister, free of the heaviness, I would have chosen it every single time. Moving forward, I want to honor that bond we have shared, not by rewriting the past but by respecting where each of us is now, even when it's been difficult over the years. You will continue to carve out a space in the world that is uniquely yours—filled with your talent, artistry, and spirit. I hope joy and fulfillment follow you wherever you go.

If you ever find yourself watching two little girls spinning on a merry-go-round, I hope you think of us—and smile. Here is to courage, healing and possibly finding our way back when we are both ready.

With Love, SHC

Dad, I have truly done my best to support Shiloh—with love, patience and both emotional and financial backing. I have shown up for her through her struggles, listened without judgment and offered what I could from the heart. And yet, it often feels like its never enough.

What I want is connection. I want a sister, a teammate—not the tension and distance that now defines our relationship. I am trying to find a path forward that protects my peace while still holding space for the possibility of repair. That means setting healthier boundaries and acknowledging the consistent absence of appreciation, accountability, or even common courtesy in her actions towards me.

I don't want to be petty by listing all the small things I have tolerated over the years -things that, on their own, might seem insignificant, but over time have chipped away at my sense of worth in this relationship.

It is exhausting.

And then there is Mom. She continues to play both sides, refusing to acknowledge what is going on. In doing so, she enables the dysfunction. I guess, in some ways, I have too—by trying to keep the peace, by staying quiet at times by hoping it would all somehow work itself out. I wonder what you would say to her, Dad. I wish you were here to make sense of it. I know I am not perfect and have owned my part openly and consistently. I have shared my shortcomings, my intentions and my feelings. But here I am left facing someone who won't meet me in that same spirit. She avoids direct conversation, dodges accountability, and con-tinues to view me through a lens I do not recognize.

I am tired.

I am not giving up on love. I just know I can't keep doing this at the cost of myself.

love, Me

Dear Dad,

I've spent so many years trying to find myself, but I don't feel any closer now than I did when I left home and moved into that little garden level apartment in Saginaw with Mauve carpeting.

I volunteered as a Hospice patient caregiver for ten years and started a Supper Club program to deliver meals to patients and their families. I was a board member for two years on the Women's Legacy Fund of Ventura Community Foundation and met women in the community who were doing amazing things.

I really never had role models, but I've met women who have demonstrated leadership and empowered me and helped me build my confidence. I realized others have navigated similar paths or challenges. They were able to offer practical advice and emotional support, which I was in dire need of receiving.

Aside from the trailblazing women I met within our bedroom community in Camarillo, my two neighbors Ruth in her late sixties and Madaline in her eighties provided an intergenerational friendship that fostered mutual understanding and enriched my life in ways I could not have imagined. Dad, they guided me during yet another tough time in my life, as I started having uncomfortable conversations with Mom about growing up and motherhood. During this time, I had two toddlers and the tapestry of the past was weaving into the present and I was struggling.

Dad, the gift of girlfriends has been priceless for me. There are many influential women in my life who have offered me a deeper understanding of myself through our shared storylines.

My ride-or-die girlfriend Danette has weathered some incredibly tough times. Her husband, much like you—charismatic and beloved by everyone—struggled behind closed doors with addiction, battling both alcohol and drugs before passing away two years ago. Danette and I also bonded over the challenges we faced with our in-laws; sharing stories made those early years slightly more bearable, knowing I wasn't alone in dealing with the narcissistic tendencies of my father-in-law.

I wish we could talk and you could maybe open up and share how alcohol had a hold on your life and whatever dependency you had on it, before the cancer took your life at thirty years old. I am noticing things I never did before. I see how Mom lived with your addiction and hid it from everyone, and the complexities that come with that. Your alcoholism during those early years really impacted Mom and every aspect of our lives. I don't blame you; I just want you to know how sad it makes me feel that you were hurting deep down and wonder how your well-being would have been should you have gotten help.

I didn't mean to go deep today, but sometimes the words just flow, and my stream of consciousness is like water, it goes where it wants to. Again, know I love you and still respect you, there is not judgment only empathy.

I am really working on mending my relationships with both Mom and Shiloh too. There is never a balanced view of how someone perceives their pain, but I want them both to know that I did my best in taking responsibility for ensuring their safety once you died, even if it was not smooth in the shielding process. The safe space I tried to provide was more advocacy, and standing up for what I felt was right and what we needed as they were unable to do it for themselves and you were gone. And you keep learning, Dad—there has been no shortage of crises. But I will admit something, I am done carrying the weight of keeping this family together.

Somehow, that role landed on me, and I took it on for far too long.

I have also decided to write to BJ. She deserves to know the truth. I did not hide it to be deceptive or dishonest, but because I wanted to protect her from a reality that felt too heavy at the time. I did not want to tarnish her view of her father.

But I can't keep carrying the burden of silence—not anymore.

Dear BJ,

I've been reflecting on how much you mean to me, and I want you to know, first and foremost, that I adore you. Your bright, perky personality and your impeccable sense of style have always stood out, but it's the way you bring joy and light into every moment that I treasure most.

We've shared many incredible memories—from dancing the jig in that lively pub in Dingle, Ireland, to our fireside chats in that hut in Africa. I think about those evenings with Caymus and perch at Boone's in Sutton's Bay, laughing and being silly together as the sun set on another perfect day. The list is endless, and so are the memories we've created. Every moment has left a lasting imprint on my heart.

But I need to share something with you, and it's not easy to say. For years, I kept quiet about your dad's behavior because I thought I was protecting you. I didn't want you to feel the pain or confusion that I had experienced, so I stayed silent. But now, I realize that hiding the truth isn't the way forward.

I know this may hurt, and I am deeply sorry if it does. I never wanted to cause you pain. But you deserve to know what truly happened, and I no longer wish to keep those walls between us. Please know that none of this changes the way I feel about you. You've always been, and will always be, someone I deeply care about and love, as well as my baby sister. If you ever want to talk—whether about the past or simply to reminisce about our endless adventures—I'm here for you, now and always.

Take all the time you need to process this, and know I will be by your side, no matter what.

With all my love, SHC

Dad, I hope my sisters are able to see that I've only ever tried to do what was best for all of us. It wasn't always easy and I don't know that I did what was right, but I did try.

I hope they know that.

love, me

Dear Dad,

I started a gathering of women and named it Living Legacies of Ventura County (LLVC). It's a quarterly parlor series for ladies, and each occasion presents a different topic and trailblazer from the community sharing her story in my home. They lead the discussion and share their life experiences. It is not a lecture series. Nobody wants to be told what to do. All the conversations we have are hinged on individual strengths and meant to be life discussions that provide information and camaraderie. All of which

I missed out on and longed for. Maybe it's selfish, but these intimate social gatherings have been a blast. They are more than kitchen table chit chats. We have wine, snacks and the ladies who participate are dynamic dames, let me tell you. Our first two were phenomenal women. Mary Leavens Schwabauer, who I met on the Women's Legacy Board. This woman is a visionary leader, stellar wife and mother, a teacher for thirty plus years and had been an incredible mentor to me and many others. The second speaker survived the Holocaust with her mother. She has lived eighty-six years, and her life experiences were chronicled in a book, "I Am Still Here, My Mother's Voice." I have other women on the schedule including Tristen Vance who is a licensed Marriage and Family Therapist.

She not only has been my trusted therapist and friend, but she also works with children at a shelter in Camarillo called Casa Pacifica, which help abused and neglected children.

What can I say Dad? I am not going to act like my past hasn't happened and talk about how much I hurt from it. What I decided to do is move forward and Tristen once said, "You can't heal the pain I refuse to heal," so I keep flipping my focus and no longer avoiding the pain … leaving Numbville for good…and turning my wounds into wisdom. I know you are smiling in the sky right now.

love, me

Dear Dad,

Life offered an opportunity for us as a family to move back to
Del Mar. Both boys had loved spending summers there growing
up. Cole is a freshman in High School now and Cody is in eighth
grade. We joked Cody surfed the Pacific while Cole surfed the
World Wide Web. They both were willing to pack up and move.

The boys, Dad, are true gentlemen. You would be so proud,
not just of what they do, but of who they are becoming. They
are thoughtful, funny and kind. You would laugh for hours with
them; their banter is quick, clever, and full of brotherly mischief.
They each have their own rhythm. Cole, ever curious and always
diving deep into his ideas and entrepreneurial spirit to include
his love of travel. Cody has this magnetic energy, fiercely loyal,
wild-hearted, and intuitive with that fearless love for life. Watching them grow into themselves has been my greatest joy.

This move will stretch them in new ways, I know. But they
have already shown how resilient they are, how grounded and
adaptable too. I often imagine us all sitting together, catching up,
laughing. I would grill steaks, twice-baked potatoes, and make
your favorite Boston Cream Pie. Someone would inevitably
belch or fart and blame the other, it's just how we roll. The silli-
ness is never in short supply here, and now, we get to carry that
same joy into a new house by the beach.

Tim would be driving two and a half hours one way to the
ranch, which would mean he would stay there for a few nights
leaving me and the boys. For me it meant leaving my mentees
and the emotional support I was receiving. Even so, I knew in my
heart of hearts it was the right decision.

love, me

October 2014 to December 2023
My Forties

Dear Dad,

We moved back to Del Mar where it all started.

It took a few months to find a home, but we found one on the same street where Tim and I had lived for three years after we met. Great memories have taken place in Del Mar, and I'm looking forward to making new ones.

I started a foundation to support women in a book I wrote called *S.H.E.*, and others of all ages and cultures to promote positive change in their lives through education and career development. Like LLVC, but in a book format—interesting people sharing inspiring stories.

I believe every story has meaning and purpose, whether written or spoken. I have always felt close to storytellers in my life, especially Grandma Rosie. Some of my best memories are cuddling on the coach nestled safely under the support of her arm.

These experiences of being nurtured by someone left a permanent mark on my heart. A bond was created that no one could replace. When I reflect on those times, I realized how they provided me with countless lessons and to date, this is what storytelling does for me.

I noticed that when I peeled back my layers and shared my trauma, others were emboldened to do the same. The only way I could release myself from my emotional struggles was to allow others to witness the most complicated and hidden parts of myself.

My desire to empower myself and other women was certainly rooted in watching Mom live her life from what I assumed was a position of weakness. I started becoming more and more passionate about liberating her and others like her from their imprisoned way of thinking.

As Mom slowly revealed her untold stories, I began to understand that this woman was not weak, which was how I had always perceived her, but primarily a victim of social circumstance.

I have to admit, Dad, my perception of you has changed quite a bit.

Mom told me she constantly walked on eggshells, living in fear of saying or doing something that might trigger an aggressive response from you. She didn't have the strength to remove herself from your relationship. Plus, living in Reese did not help matters. This had to be extremely difficult for her.

Growing up, I was aware there was tension between my you and Mom, but I learned how intense it had actually been. Mom had done everything she could to conceal your alcoholic outbursts and the physical abuse that she endured over the course of your twelve-year marriage.

I wonder if other family members saw her struggles, and why they didn't intervene or try to help. No one ever talked about the abusiveness you demonstrated when alcohol was in your veins.

Abuse doesn't always happen overtly, and it isn't always easy to recognize. Destructive relationships can be quite covert and insidious, and this is where I am going to have the harder conversation with you, Dad.

Over time, and with more than a couple of therapy sessions, I realized not everyone is ready to be vulnerable at a moment's notice. I understand that more now than ever. That is one of the reasons why I wrote *S.H.E. Share Heal Empower*. I want to whisper quietly in the readers ear and my own, that they are not alone. When they are ready, they will find innumerable women to draw closer to, be in relationship with, and confide in.

I frequently asked myself how Mom could be honest without tarnishing the love I had of my adored father during our conversations. I respect her selflessness in keeping my memories of you pure. Yet it still pains my heart to realize she became an expert in silent suffering for the sake of other people, especially Shiloh and me.

I was glad to give her an opportunity to use her voice after being silent for so long. It did. Allowing Mom to free herself, find resolution within, and step forward with a newfound strength makes me extraordinarily happy. Mom's incredible courage inspired me to want to share, heal, and empower. This book became my opportunity to do that.

I wrote down Mom's entire chapter for you to read, starting with my introduction and then Mom sharing her story:

> *My courageous mother's past continues to influence my fervent interest in the empowerment of women. My vision is to amplify not only my mother's voice, but also all women's voices, both individually and collectively, helping them (and me) realize our power, understand our greatness, and model that strength for our children and grandchildren.*

We all keep secrets, sometimes for good reasons, and sometimes because we are ashamed of things that happen behind closed doors. Being heard matters; it is how we turn our wounds into wisdom.

My mother has always been a giver, a pattern that most of us as women naturally adopt. Frequently, she gave at great cost to herself. For me, I want her to finally be heard here in my book, and I am proud to use her story as the final chapter.

Like so many mother/daughter relationships, ours was often fraught with misunderstanding. As a teenager, I thought she was weak, so I continually confronted her for not standing up to her second husband, whom I despised. I didn't respect her choices, or support how she cowered to both his daily demands and his emotional abuse. What I viewed as a lack of self-respect agitated me tremendously. I was too emotionally immature at the time to understand the complexity of my mother's situation. I forgive her now, in hindsight.

Over the years, I began to ask intense questions of her, since I suspected buried secrets. My mother, when she was ready to face her past, provided the deep, gut-wrenching answers that I was searching for in my mid-twenties. Little did I know the silent suffering she endured as a young wife and mother. Over the years, she muddled stories from my youth to protect the image I carried of my father, who passed away from cancer when I was eleven.

As she frequently says, "No one knows what goes on inside your home until they sit at your dinner table." Our

interview for this book is the first time she has fully dis-
closed the conflict that went on with my father over forty
years ago. Throughout my life, my mother handled some of
the hardest hits that life could throw at her, yet she some-
how managed to spring back again and again.

The truth is that within my mother Joni, a soundless
strength has always resided. In my thirties, I learned to be
gentler with my judgment, recognizing she was doing what
she could with what she had, and in the only way she knew
how. She has always given freely of herself, without expec-
tations, and the respect she has for others is evidenced by
her desire to help them achieve their potential. Giving and
accepting are my mother's trademarks of genuine caring
and love.

As a mother myself, I now recognize that the job of moth-
ering is very complex and difficult. We try to protect our
family however we can, no matter what. Sometimes
silence is best; other times, that same silence can be the
entry into an uncommunicative prison. My mother has
mentioned several times that being a mother comes with
second guessing everything you're doing (or not doing),
and then wondering if what you did will, in some way,
scar your child for life.

I love my mother's gigantic, generous heart, along with
her ability to spark up a conversation with complete
strangers in a matter of minutes, a vital communication
skill she has mastered over the last four decades as a hair
stylist. Could this natural talent for communication have
been better utilized within our family system when I was

growing up? I really don't know the true answer to that question, yet perhaps most importantly, my mother is using that talent now.

Sharing our stories can always be a step toward freedom; so can making our own decisions, following our hearts, and speaking our truth. My mother taught me these realities by modeling what to do, as well as what not to do. I am full of pride and tremendously grateful as her daughter. I am also elated to be her biggest advocate, watching her rebuild not only her life, but her confidence as well.

Dad, this is Mom's version of her story—shared for the first time ever—in the final chapter of the book:

JONI

I wasn't what you would call one of the popular girls in my high school. The "cool" status was for cheerleaders; sometimes I was jealous of not being one. But I saw myself as friendly and carefree. I could fit in with all types of people, yet never liked to draw too much attention to myself. I was a bit self-conscious and not a big drinker.

You could either find me at band practice with my cornet, or in yearbook and student council meetings after school.

Tom Hogan worked at the local market, the IGA. I remember watching him bag our fruits and vegetables, being captivated by his hazel eyes. We went to the same high school, and we would flirt with each other while he loaded groceries into my mom's ivy green Ford Mustang. I started going to the baseball games to watch him play shortstop, his wavy light brown hair barely contained under his ball cap.

Tom had a big heart. Everybody loved him. He was charismatic, good looking, and the life of the party. He even drank enough Budweiser for both of us! We started going steady the fall of our junior year. I was thrilled to be going to our Spring Senior Prom together!

In the summer of 1973, the whole course of my life changed. Who knew I would unexpectedly conceive the first time I had sex, parked in the sugar beet field on a muggy summer night in Tom's two-door Plymouth. I was a wreck. Mom accompanied me to our family doctor, and he confirmed my pregnancy with a urine test. The thought of telling my father scared me to death.

When I finally did, he refused to talk to me for two months.

I was only seventeen. I was never taught either at home or in school about sex, let alone the need to wear protection or use contraceptives! It was a different time in the '70s. I had to learn all the "physical and emotional stuff" on my own. After the shock subsided, there was never a thought of abortion or adoption. Tom's family was Catholic and mine, Lutheran. I'm not sure if I would have considered either option even if religion was not a definitive factor. In our small town, if you got pregnant, you got married and dealt with it.

My hopes of going to college and becoming a nurse or a dental hygienist instantly came to a halt. Instead, I attended MJ Murphy Cosmetology School. The smell of perm solution fumes made me feel sick to my stomach on a daily basis; maybe it was just morning sickness. I'll never know.

We were married on December 7, 1973. To appease Tom's father and his family, the wedding was held at his Catholic Church. I wore an off-white empire waist wedding dress to hide my five-month bump, carrying an intensely fragrant stephanotis flower bouquet. Two hundred people came to the reception. I felt excited and optimistic as our real-life version of playing house together began.

Fortunately, my father's disappointment waned. He liked Tom and helped us purchase a $7,000, fully furnished, white-trimmed trailer home. We could barely afford our utility bills, but to Tom and me this prefabricated, two-bedroom structure felt like a residence for royalty! We ate boiled boloney and fried eggs for dinner on our gold butterfly Corelle dishes. From time to time, Tom would go hunting or fishing and bring back squirrel, pheasant, rabbit, or blue gills for me to prepare for dinner.

My new husband was working his way up the ranks at the IGA, but he still found plenty of time for partying. At that time, it was easy for me to make the excuse that he was young, but I was, too! I found my first job at Jarvis Hair Salon in Saginaw six months later. The goal was to save up money for the arrival of our child, and we desperately needed my additional income.

Our baby girl, Shannon, arrived in April 1974.

We could have saved more money, but Tom's drinking never diminished. I had reasonable expectations of him as a father. I wanted him to stop drinking every night and stay home with his family. Then together we would navigate through the uncertainly that comes with being parents.

When he refused, my high hopes of living happily ever after with my newlywed husband and newborn child started to seem in jeopardy. Here I was, a teenager, alone, desperately trying my best to take care of the house, our finances, and a newborn without a parenting manual. Tom's routine was consistent: He would drink at the bar without stopping until he either passed out or never came home, or he would come home just *before* passing out.

Each month his behavior became more intolerable. Since I never knew where he was, it worried me sick. I spent countless hours pacing the floors in darkness with Shannon crying softly in my arms, asking myself, why am I doing this? Even as a teenage mother, I knew I had to be responsible for my actions, and I needed to be there for my daughter.

I was reluctant to accept what was happening, and was hopeful Tom would stop his childish behavior. My pride took precedence over my wisdom. My fear of failure and embarrassment petrified me. I didn't reach out to anyone since

I thought people would not believe me. I protected Tom's reputation at all costs, at my expense. I felt so alone though, never telling anyone about the situation I found myself in, stuffing my feelings down deeper and deeper.

At a certain point during the first year of our marriage, Tom started to get explosive toward me when he came home drunk. My fun-loving husband turned combative the moment I asked him, "Where have you been?" I never knew what the "alcohol" was going to say or do. Sometimes I would have a mouthful of chewed-up tuna fish sandwich spit at me, or I might need to dodge a full glass of milk that would end up shattered against the kitchen wall. Retreating to my hands and knees, I would start to clean up the mess while begging him to go to bed. Yet anything I said or did aggravated his teenage angst.

Two years prior, Mom gave me one of my favorite gifts from a trip she and Dad took to Hawaii. It was a beige and white cotton caftan dress. I was wearing it one night while ironing in the living room when Tom came home in a drunken stupor and ripped it off me. I vividly remember sitting there on the navy-blue tweed carpet holding my shredded dress in my hands, weeping. I continued to softly cry as I cleaned up another one of his spontaneous food-throwing fits. He finally staggered to the bedroom, where he promptly passed out.

For years, I lived in continual fear of him walking through the front door, dreading what would happen next. After so many nights of his nastiness, I decided that I would no longer wait up. My new plan was to pretend I was asleep. This idea was short-lived. My strategy failed when he pointed a shotgun to my left temple as I lay in bed one night and sternly demanded, "You always have to say something to me when I walk in the door," as he pushed the unsympathetic steel barrel against my skin.

My body trembled. My brain seized. I tried to remain calm, but his shaky right hand made me feel extremely nervous that I was going to die. I prayed to God this firearm was not loaded. My drunken, emotionless husband should not be the one to make the decision to end my life.

And especially not with my little girl peacefully sleeping on her favorite Raggedy Ann and Andy doll sheets and cuddling her faded pink blankie in the next room.

I was aware of Tom's incapacity to listen when he was intoxicated, but I also knew that anything could set him off. So in that moment I asked him calmly, "Do you really want to do this? If you pull the trigger, then you have to live with that decision." He eventually put the gun down and went to bed. I ran to my little girl's room and held her as close as I could, all the while asking God, "Why me?"

What could I do now? Where could I go? Back to my parents' house? They already thought being pregnant at seventeen was an embarrassment to them. There were no services or shelters available in our small town. I could have called the police and exposed Tom's behavior, but nobody would have believed me, especially our friends and family. He never acted this crazy in front of them. Everyone liked and loved Tom Hogan.

I am not sure why I stayed after that traumatic night, but I did. I would like to confess that things settled down a bit, but as I look back, my decision was mostly fear-based. Two years after that incident, our second daughter, Shiloh, was born. I did not want seven-year-old Shannon to be an only child, and it felt like it was now or never to conceive again.

Around this time, we moved out of the trailer into a house with a yard. Tom enjoyed having a garage where he kept all his "toys." Our new house was close to the IGA so he could walk to work. He seemed excited about our new place, and I loved watching him playfully interact with the girls. He was a doting dad.

Still, over time I lost whatever assertiveness and confidence I had left in me. I continued to repress my thoughts and feelings, becoming more desensitized. Tom was physically abusive to me. I didn't want to admit to anyone what was happening in my life, and, as a result, I became a victim of my own circumstances. I talked myself in circles because I was ashamed. Was I "right" to feel the way I did? Was I supposed to suffer? Everything I thought was wrong about my relationship then started to feel "right." At least I knew what it looked like; everything was familiar and predictable, which made it comfortable somehow. I thought about leaving Tom all the time, but I was trapped by my pride and fear.

I became adept at making excuses for my bumps and bruises to friends and family. I remember one particular time that tactic was a bit more difficult, though. Tom had punched me in the mouth, causing my teeth to cut through my lip.

This happened during the middle of the night, and Shannon walked in as I was hunched over a blood-filled bathtub. I told her, "Go back to bed. Mommy slipped on some ice." I lied to my friend Carleen with the same story, while we shared a green olive pizza for lunch the next day.

Tom never laid a finger on the girls, only me. He was a good dad and loved his daughters. And I know he loved me, too. But when he drank, he became a different person. Alcohol fueled an angry fire inside of him. The more he drank, the nastier he would get. Like a fire, his actions were difficult to anticipate, and when left unattended, could quickly get out of control. That scared me.

In my mind, I thought maybe it was my fault, that I was the cause of his abusive behavior. I know now that is the furthest thing from the truth, but I was young, naive and foolish. Something I regret never saying to Tom was, "You need help." His dad was also an alcoholic; like Tom, he never knew when to stop. Drinking was an accepted behavior in their family. It was also what many people did socially in our isolated community.

It may be wrong to think, but at times I wished him dead. I was angry and tired, and I just wanted Tom to stop drinking and stop hurting me. From the beginning, I was frustrated that he did not care enough to come home and be with his family.

I desperately tried to remind him of his responsibilities, but that only aggravated his temper. When we exchanged vows, this was not the life I had envisioned.

There was a kind and loving side to Tom, but alcohol slithered in and stole that away. I wanted my Tom back, the one with the captivating hazel eyes who brought me home damaged cans of corn and green beans from work. Since we were always short on money, anything helped. Those little gifts meant a lot.

Shannon was nine and Shiloh had turned two when Tom started having severe headaches, coupled with stiffness in his neck. The headaches were odd to me, since he never used to get them, even after his drinking binges. He visited a chiropractor and took vitamins, but the symptoms didn't get better. After developing a severe cough and seeing a physician, he was finally diagnosed with a rare form of non-Hodgkin lymphoma.

Maybe I was being young and foolish again, but I never thought about him dying, or being by myself raising two girls. I only hoped that this would be the tipping point so he would finally stop drinking.

He did.

Tom endured almost two years of both chemotherapy and radiation treatments. He was sober the whole time, due in part to the severity of his sickness. I felt like God had finally answered my prayers. This was the first time in our relationship that I saw my husband daily. I knew where he was at all times. I drove him to his chemotherapy and radiation visits. We would often stop and get Jamocha milkshakes from Arby's, which helped ease his queasiness.

Our time together began to feel like a true marriage, despite his being very ill. He would play baseball with Shiloh in the back-yard and take Shannon up north to drive the quads he bought with his brother and nephew. We would go golfing together, and I would fry one of his favorite foods, either venison or fresh perch. It felt like we were renewing our relationship and starting over again. He was turning back into the Tom Hogan I fell in love with a decade earlier.

He continued to work at the grocery store when he could and started attending a non-denominational Bible study with an old high school friend, Tony. After reading the entire Bible several times, Tom appeared calmer, kinder and more caring towards me, despite the cancerous tumor resting between his lungs on his spinal cord. This inoperable malignant growth eventually made its way into his bones, taking over his entire body.

I was sitting next to my thirty-year-old husband when he peacefully closed his eyes and passed away on August 30, 1985. A non-dramatic, eerie silence filled the room. When Tom took his final breath, part of me died with him. I was now numb and emotionally empty. We had experienced many tumultuous years of marriage. But suddenly, my whole life felt like a bigger mess.

I had no time to feel scared or sorry for myself. I knew I had to be strong for Shannon and Shiloh, now ages eleven and four. There were a multitude of bills to pay and affairs to settle. I did what I needed to do...get through each day. As long as I had my girls to raise, giving up would never be an option for me.

Thanks to my older daughter, this secret is no longer buried. I had never revisited these events until she forced me to look back and tell her about my life. It has been painful, even humiliating at times, but our conversations were therapeutic as well. Unearthing these memories allows me to finally heal that part of me. In truth, to this day I still struggle with remaining silent, not saying what I really think.

I know deep in my heart this suppression is wrong, but it is a hard habit to break after a lifetime of restraint.

Now at sixty-two, I am finally taking steps toward expressing my own voice again in order to find a place of overall health and happiness. I am restoring my self-confidence, while battling type 1 diabetes. I try to visit my four grandchildren in California as much as I can, while keeping my cosmetology clients happy. My older regulars are adamant about having their hair styled on schedule—some weekly, others every six weeks. I am happily married again to a man who likes Fruity Pebbles and is a girls' high school basketball coach. Richard Carroll has been a walk in the park compared to my first two marriages. I'm grateful he actually enjoys doing the laundry and dishes, and we manage to have fun doing life together.

Slowly but surely, I am finally understanding that I deserve to be happy. My daughter continues to prod, poke, and pull me to a different level of awareness. At times, I wish she would just leave me alone! Yet in reality, *her* strength has risen from *my* past weakness. That resiliency is a gift any mother would gladly suffer to give her children.

Dad, I do hope you are proud of Mom. I am.

When Mom finally shared her side of the story and it was published, many of the relatives were furious.

In fact, to date, those same ones have not talked to me and think I have disgraced you. At first, I had a hard time accepting their denial. They weren't present and didn't hear or see what I did. At the time, I didn't understand, but I do now. I gave Mom her freedom of expression to help others come out of silence.

You are my dad, and I love you, always will. Your behavior when you were drunk was unacceptable. For that, I want others to learn that being open and vulnerable toward family secrets is the only way to heal and help.

Dad, I want you to know this "family secret" was done not only delicately and not meant to paint you as the villain but rather as someone who had flaws, like the rest of us. Sharing was necessary for the well-being of myself, Mom, and others. The motivation was to educate and empower, not eradicate relationships. I cannot control how relatives reacted and make it less than what really happened.

All my life, I take pride in being direct, yet sensitive when sharing information to anyone and being straightforward with my feelings. Always compassionate and considerate knowing it may be difficult.

I wanted to have a discussion with them, but they chose not to and cut me out of their lives.

What the S.H.E. community and the dozens of women who shared their stories, as well as many others, have taught me that we are all wounded, we all worry, and we are all weighed down by our feelings of unworthiness. For me, the bedrock of love, friendship, and community is vulnerability. Heartfelt exchanges can provide us with connection and consolation since we all long to be loved.

I wish you could respond. Maybe show me a sign, like a deer or a bird appearing at my window to let me know you understand.

love, me

January 2022 to May 2024

Late Forties & First Months of Being Fifty

Dear Dad,

For far too long, I wanted closure. I wanted an apology. I wanted to be told I mattered or thanked for being strong.

Being hurt by those close to me was painful and some acted as if it never happened. I realize all families are dysfunctional, and the passing of time does not make the hurt go away.

I learned with Tim's family that not having open conversations and apologizing are adults simply avoiding accountability. I have also heard from members of my own family to "just get over it" or "stop living in the past." I would love to, but time does not heal all issues or wounds.

My body remembers. Pain lives in every cell within me, regardless of time. Addressing the pain is the only thing that has healed me.

I need closure but too many people just want to pretend bad things didn't happen.

I spent far too much of my life pleading my case, overexplaining myself, and desperately seeking people who have hurt me to acknowledge what they have done and apologize for it. However, the more I do this, the more helpless I feel. I do not want to be invalidated and invisible, but it's been a blessing to finally see that these people who have wronged me—Shiloh included—are incapable of taking accountability. Mom and I have been nothing short of honest with each other, for that I am thankful.

My therapist Tristen, recently told me in a session, "They are just showing their emotional capacity."

This revelation was empowering. I now know I don't need closure or an apology to heal. I only need self-compassion, self-validation, and support from people who "get" me. It has taken me a long time to realize that many of the people in the past who have hurt me either can't apologize or will never own the role they played. All I can do is show myself grace and belief in a better future with more wisdom.

I hope someday I will be able to forgive and move on.

love, me

Dear Dad,

I wrote another piece for myself and then read it to Tim's stepmother right before the holiday. I just can't take the weight anymore of holding both families together when all I wanted was a community of loving people on all sides. My main focus moving forward will be my marriage and being a mom to Cole and Cody.

Here is what I told her one-night fireside:

> I have been watching this family flail forward for years. I have filled gaps and tried to not only help by showing love and bringing my light but also preserve the family dynamic, encouraging communication and vulnerability,

and basic relationship skills. All while attempting to keep my own family intact & prove that love and light are more powerful than darkness & dependency.

Yet somehow, through the years, over twenty—I became the outsider, the villain, an antagonist who stirred the pot, disrupted the system, and made people accountable for their actions while defending myself. I was tagged as a taker and user when the money never mattered to me— my children and I would have had the same life with or without the funds (smaller homes, fewer vacations, etc.). Still, they would always have had me as their mother, who fought tirelessly for their well-being and loved them uncon-ditionally for who they are. It's funny how I am considered the one who keeps causing problems in this family. Isn't it—me? The one who entered after everyone was fully formed and has been the only person "modeling" noth-ing but kindness, compassion, and forgiveness at my own expense to those who have not earned or deserved it.

Not anymore. No longer will I live a lie, a masked illusion of what this "family" is not—I am stopping the pretending. It has been far too long with me "doing good for the greater whole." All of you, including my father-in-law, have for years officially lost my trust and respect… and to be clear, "you et al." have the relationship you have with the boys because of me—I made sure to protect them from the nas-tiness, and manipulative ways of this family. They are kind to you because of me and the experiences that shaped them with others in the world when I could have very easily have allowed them to see you for what you are. I didn't do that because I had empathy for you, as undeserved as that was.

I knew that if I did not shield them, they would very likely have "despised" you and "distanced" our family from you and or my father-in-law.

The gig is up. I am no longer facilitating this relationship. I will be polite and neighborly, but the "fluff" is gone. I knew my worth and belonging when I entered this family. After betraying myself for far too long and attempting to fit into this family to accept manipulation and vindictiveness; to go against all I know to be right, good, and kind.

I am done negotiating with people who do not respect or see what I have done for the greater good. I know you are incapable of that without being told. Even when I had shared with you over the years "how to handle" or "what not to do," you still did the opposite and shunned me versus stand up for me or with me.

In short, I will no longer look aside to being treated as an outsider, villain, or enemy. I resign from that role. Through all the toxicity over the years, the one thing I have always had is my sense of self. It has served me well and guided me as a mother. I can't change this family's ways, but I know I can care for my family and, most importantly, myself.

After reading this to step-mother-in-law out loud, I felt lighter.

I feel she was strongly influenced by Tim's late father and frequently shared his perspectives, at her own expense.

His father passed in November of 2022, leaving many messes to clean up. By unmasking myself for the final time, I shared my continued contempt towards certain behaviors, which are still in the process of changing. However, extracting this brought me closure to a lingering and arduous 2023. Moving forward and knowing, I am no longer settling for a tolerable level of contentment for the greater whole and playing the game within this dysfunctional family system I married into – as I had my own to deal with. The reason I decided to read this to her was based on many toxic situations where I was finally fed up with not being protected by my husband and him taking accountability of his reality. This last year of my life taught me a lot and I don't deserve to be the one always doing the protecting and pretending its all okay. I believe authenticity is vital. I needed her to have full transparency moving forward if we were to redefine our relationship. The liberation was needed just like it was with Mom and Shiloh. As I started to sift through the shit of others, I began realizing it wasn't mine to be a container for. I have my own trauma triggers.

My heartfelt intent over the years has been to simply inform Tim of the injustice I continue to feel within his family. Do I blame Tim, yes at times, as he has not stepped up and supported me in front of them. He had become numb to the behavior of his dad, that is his story to tell, but it sure has affected me and our children.

I choose safety over independence with our marriage. Meaning we agreed early, he would protect me financially, as I opted to quit my corporate career to raise our children and build a foundation within our family that he nor I had growing up. I struggle with reconciling my resentment toward him for not being more verbal.

Yet, I do understand why. Adulting is hard.

love, me

Dear Dad,

I feel like I have been stuck in a loop, reliving the past and struggling to move forward, no matter how hard I try. The past ten years have felt like I'm living in a cycle of dysfunction.

I have always written to you as a way to make sense of my feelings and the world around me. I want to share with others how my trauma froze me at the age it happened. It has taken me years to unpack this. A part of me is still living in the past, yet I feel like the suffering is happening right now. Trauma, death, divorce, or abandonment doesn't just happen, and then it's over. These experiences affected me in different ways throughout life until I finally did the work to heal. Understanding my emotional quicksand syndrome has been a game-changer.

As I learned to heal my wounds and bring the inner child back to being seen and heard, loving her, and holding her heart, I rebuilt the trust within myself—a type of rewiring of loving myself and not looking to others to love me.

I needed to love myself; everyone else's love was ancillary. I needed to reflect and celebrate the small victories and milestones in my healing journey, which reinforced the positivity inside, and having the breakthrough of how hard I have navigated this way back to myself has been. Still, I have done it by expressing my vulnerabilities and working through my trauma. Which created a deep bond with my younger self and who I am today.

Trust me on this. I continue to make peace with my past and move forward in the present, but reminding the younger part of me that she is no longer running the show.

I wrote another piece in January and published it and wanted to include it for you to read, the title is "Striving for More:"

Tapping into who we are and what we want from life is no easy undertaking. There are myriads of obstacles that can stop us in our tracks at various points—significant events that can change the course of our life in entirely unpredictable ways, as well as everyday life events that simply pile upon one another until we feel we are completely burdened and immobilized by their weight. I know that all too well in my own life.

Finding our authentic selves is a journey that often requires years of work and reflection that not everyone is keen to embrace. It's easier sometimes to sit in what is, to not question, to not wonder, to not rock the proverbial boat, to accept what comes our way without regard to our well-being or desires. I have always fought this resignation, though not as successfully and valiantly as I may have always hoped, ultimately falling back on old habits and acceptances that left me feeling empty.

And yet, regardless of how low my lows may have been at various times in my life, I am a seeker. Self-discovery has always been my North Star. I thrive on deciphering my feelings, addressing my reactions, and assessing my awareness of the world. It's my way of finding my way.

In 2023, this need for self-discovery became more profound than ever. After twenty-five years of attempting to hold my marriage together, which left me feeling alone on an island, not to mention emotionally exhausted from carrying my husband and his "generational gook." I had arrived at an impasse. I was tired of trying to course correct for myself while at the same time trying to right the family dynamic that has hung over us like a black cloud for decades. I was no longer okay with this dynamic being at my expense.

I had finally realized that the energy I offered was given too freely.

Things came to a head mid-year, which led to several events that genuinely didn't settle within me until the turn of the new year. It's somewhat ironic that it landed at such a traditional time. Each January marks the beginning of a new year, an opportunity to lay the past to rest and look to the future. And, if willing to do so, a time to reflect. The name "January" is derived from the Roman God, Janus, who was said to have two faces—one looking to the past and one looking to the future. He was the god of doors, gates, and transitions. And, wow, did Janus ever live up to his name?!

I am still collecting my thoughts and takeaways from all that transpired this past year. My need to assemble them in a fluid fashion has been challenging, yet never before have I known how important it was for me to do so. It was crystal clear to me that while I had undergone a year of dodging punches, it was also a year of formidable endurance—a year in which I stuck to my moral framework and, as a result, discovered profound lessons in relearning and unlearning who I am and what I want to continue to put out in the world. As a lover of wordsmithing, resilience became my word.

While I am ready to close last year's chapter—the final year of my forties—I want to take note of a few of the significant events that gave me a deeper understanding of my past, an experience that I have been searching for years to uncover; an understanding that has illuminated the opportunities I now feel I have for a new beginning. Three were particularly significant in reminding me who I am and want to be in the days, months, and years ahead.

The first of these was actually a second—the publication of my second S.H.E. book, a compilation of stories from twenty-three women of all ages and cultures who courageously share their heartfelt journeys of discovery, resilience, and perseverance. At first, I resisted the pull to write a second book but relented when I realized I had more stories that needed sharing, voices that deserved to be heard. In taking this leap, I recognized that these women, like the twenty-two featured in my first book, are beacons of light that have helped illuminate my path of discovery—the power I possess. This year, working with a new editor— one proven to be my girl guru in many ways beyond this book—brought greater understanding to this storytelling journey of mine: we find bits and pieces of ourselves in others, like pieces of a magical mosaic that can help us better define ourselves and strengthen our journeys.

So, this first event (realization, really) was impactful. It proved that my long-held belief in the power and healing nature of storytelling is something I know I need to honor.

The second event in 2023 came on the heels of the publication of volume two of my book. This year-long effort culminated in an art gallery event showcasing the works of art that twenty-four artists explicitly created for the featured stories. It was a beautiful celebration of an accomplishment I felt very proud to have completed. Yet, as full as this made me feel, I also felt depleted of energy. How does that make sense? Feeling full and depleted at the same time?

Well, in the story of my life, I often feel like a paradox or walking contradiction. I am learning it's fairly universal; many of the women I interviewed for my books reminded me that I am not alone in this feeling. We are not alone. It's okay to, at times, feel like a dichotomy of contradiction, to feel a push and pull that can seem out of step with the attempts of this push and pull to co-exist. It reminds you that you have dimension, depth, and resources for growth. What I realized, however, was that my feelings of being spent extended far beyond the publication of my book and a simple sense of unrest. It developed deep into my relationships. Being busy simply masked the extent of those borders. When the dust of activity finally settled, experiences I'd had and pushed aside came back to the forefront, forcing me to dig deep into my core for answers and the roots of my unrest.

Some of the many ups and downs I have experienced will be chronicled in a book. For now, I will simply say that I felt overwhelmed, too much so at times, with many situations pulling at me from many angles, asking for more and more and more… of which I had nothing more to give. I can honestly say I was at a breaking point—contemplating my purpose in matrimony and life and why my actions matter. I could no longer continue putting everyone else's needs and wants before my own, carrying other's feelings for them, allowing them to skirt their responsibilities, struggling to hold my family together, and parenting a partner who chose to avoid the demons that plagued him.

After several disastrous moments in the last four months of the year, my remarkable therapist and friend, Tristen, listened intently to my turmoil and said, "Trust yourself." Those simple words have haunted me my whole life, yet they have also driven me and been the bedrock of many sound decisions. Trusting myself has caused me to push harder, to be more verbal, and to fight against injustice.

What I trusted was that I needed to be alone. I needed to travel. Travel has been something that has been a part of my life and love since as far back as I can remember and something that I feel privileged to be able to do. As a seeker, travel provides answers and insights that might otherwise go undiscovered… gems, forever lost.

I have always turned to my love of travel in both times of joy and need, and this past year presented more of the latter.

In the past, my sanctuaries were Bali, Thailand, and other places where calm can reside within me. But this time, the idea of a road trip felt right: an opportunity to detach from the chaos I was swirling in, to give me the time and space I needed to think. I started with four- teen days in the south, traversing through six states in a rental car I coined Chrissy the Chrysler. Throughout my travels, I came to randomly meet charming folks who reminded me of my core without even knowing me. These magical moments of crossing paths are something I relish. It is what led me to embark on writing my S.H.E. books. My editor, girl guru, said it was my superpower. She noted that I had a "magnetic field" that draws people to me to share their stories openly and honestly. I do feel that people cross my path for a reason, and I'm always open to the experience.

This trip proved no different.

I met many people during those two weeks of travel. Whether sitting alone for a morning coffee or in a hotel bar for dinner, my solitude rarely remained. Short pleasantries shared with other travelers coming and going often evolved into conversation, often serving as a mirror to myself, presenting different perspectives on life that challenged my assumptions and prompted further self-reflection. While navigating unfamiliar environments and encountering new challenges, I was again reminded of my resilience and adaptability. When I have these walkabouts—my personal travels—they often lead to greater introspection, self-reflection, and engagement in activities that bring me joy and fulfillment. They always contribute to a better understanding of myself. I relish meeting new people and hearing their stories; I learn much about myself through them. Taking time away taught me that I needed to step away from social convention and what I believed the world and my loved ones needed from me. It made me realize that I needed to be a better boundary-setter in my personal life.

A few encounters I had over these two weeks were incredibly impactful.

The first took place in Charlotte, North Carolina, at a hotel bar in a far less provocative manner than that line may imply. I settled in at the bar with a glass of Caymus and a light meal, perusing a script I promised a friend I'd review when an elderly gentleman, a retired lawyer, took the stool beside me.

Making idle chitchat, he asked what I was reading. After briefly explaining, we extended our conversation to travel and vineyards, both apropos of the moment. Our discourse was easy and fluid, delving deeper into why we relish travel and time to reflect. I found our conversation touching and bizarrely awesome, neither of which I ever questioned. Ultimately, this wise octogenarian reminded me to be unapologetically myself and never settle for a tolerable level of unhappiness. What a gift! It's not that we somehow don't know this is how we should be; we sometimes need it reflected to see it. I do not question some encounters; I only glean the wisdom gained.

The second encounter that moved me was like those that inspired me to write my books—a chance encounter with a woman of resilience. This meeting took place in Beaufort, South Carolina. Again, settling into a spot at a bar for a glass of wine and dinner, I happened to sit next to a stylish woman who I quickly learned owned her interior design firm. Though successful, she shared that her life was anything but, as she was going through a divorce. She offered that the constant search for salvation in her partner of twenty years left her depleted. We spent three hours conversing, exchanging numbers, and discussing possibly including her SHERO story in a potential volume three.

The grand finale of my trek—one that moved me to the brink of nearly falling off my stool—was my chance meeting with a prominent literary figure while visiting Charleston, South Carolina. As a nonfiction writer myself, dabbling in biographies, obituaries, and personal narratives for years, fiction has been calling me, yet I keep ignoring it. After thirty minutes of platitudes—talking about family and fun—while he sipped his smoky old-fashioned and I my glass of Chablis—he very eloquently offered, "Shannon, go to the edge, then go further. There are no boundaries when it comes to writing or life." Again, we know these things to be true. Applying them to ourselves is another thing. Hearing these words somehow resonated with me in a way I don't think I might have been ready for previously.

The following night, in Savannah, Georgia, after dinner with a couple from the Hamptons I had met six months prior, I sat at the hotel rooftop bar sipping a glass of champagne, ready to retire for the evening when I met another dynamic individual: a therapist for a women's center in Naples, Florida. She shared that she is a married mother of a six-year-old boy trying to hold it all together. As our conversation unfolded, she disclosed that she deeply desired to be more adventurous and travel more. "I need more time alone and want to do uncomfortable things, but traveling solo feels scary," she whispered. As I write this, I am pinching myself, reminded of the kismet I felt swirling around me at that moment and how mindboggling it was.

Shortly after she left, I was still spiraling, thinking it may be the bubbly. I turned to my phone to check my email and found a note from the media department of Dollywood, a theme park in Pigeon Forge, Tennessee, confirming that they would be happy to host me on a private tour. I had contacted them earlier in the week, indicating my interest in writing a story on women and philanthropy. Dolly Parton is a musical icon and trailblazer for women. Her challenge of societal gender norms and efforts to break through various constructs have always inspired me. I intended to write a story on her influence as a woman philanthropist and inspiration. She is a woman who has trusted her heart and connected with the greater world community through her musical storytelling genius.

As 2023 came to a close, I felt grateful for the silence and solitude I gave myself—a space that awarded me my greatest confidant, myself. Using a Dolly expression, I "put wings on my dreams." Following my visit to Dollywood, as a means of honoring the rewarding spirit of storytelling that I believe I share with Dolly, I had the S.H.E. Foundation donate one hundred S.H.E. Share Heal Empower, Collected Journeys, Volume Two books to The Dollywood Foundation and Dolly's Imagination Library. I'm thrilled to be a small part of these organizations' inspiring efforts to promote the power of words and stories as change agents for good.

Throughout my travels, I felt overwhelmingly grateful for all my encounters, conversations, and shared stories. It took a handful of strangers to remind me who I am and how I was built. I have always been interested in what I don't know and the expansion of knowledge—trying to capture wisdom and reproduce it beneficially. Human behavior fascinates me, especially my own. I believe the signs that directed my path in life were always there, but I often doubted the direction. I had stopped listening to my inner Rosie, my inner guide that always had my back. I named this source after my paternal grandmother. I realized that ignoring her when I needed her most created a massive roadblock. This road trip and the insights I gained spurred me to make a deal with both of us not to allow this oversight to continue. I know this internal compass is essential to my growth since I am the best person to comprehend myself, my disconnects, and my desires.

This second awakening came to me via this road trip, made it clear that trusting my heart and acknowledging my desire for shared humanity through storytelling is as essential to my being as the air I breathe.

The third critical event that bubbled up is more personal—my marriage. This past year, all the chaos of an extended family that had been left unchecked for years—issues and transgressions that I always felt I was left to manage—finally came to a point where it was detrimental to my well-being. I finally realized that it was not my responsibility to carry the burdens of others. I wanted freedom from this toxicity. As a result, my husband and I had some very uncomfortable, long-overdue talks. Thankfully, he was ready to engage, to discuss the awkward truths that floated between us—both his and mine. While not easy, these conversations have brought about a more profound understanding and closeness, both of which had been missing due to a fragmented first family system he experienced and is still working to comprehend.

We have begun to create a safe space for questioning and sharing. My favorite inquiry lately has been, how close are these versions we portray of ourselves to our absolute truth? Together with my own intergenerational identity, I want to explore and be as close to my truth as possible, expressing the person I truly am without melding to whatever audience or drama is present. I no longer want to hide my multitude of layers. I no longer wish to engage in a dance of turmoil, manipulated by pain I didn't quite understand.

This final event of addressing my marital relationship was what I knew I needed to do upon my return from travel. It solidified the overarching message which became clear. I must honor myself by stepping fully into my authenticity and finding spaces and relationships where it's safe to be myself.

The events this year helped me see, feel, and understand where I need to be. I have always been in a state of flux and restructuring, but here's to a more peaceful and purposeful 2024, where I'll focus more on myself and my study of self-writing in my 'babe cave,' deconstructing myself and my discontent, and living with resilience.

love, me

Dear Dad,

I often wonder how our conversations would turn out if I came to you and asked you for communication and feeling advice.

I was so young when we were together those short eleven years. Did you have the skills? Would you have evolved or devolved like many did in my circle?

We will never know this about each other. I wish we could have gotten to know each other over the years.

Over the years, Dad, there have been endless soul-shifting lessons from living and loving that have taught me about myself and how to love my past. These experiences, with some careful distillation, have provided profound insights.

After writing to you all these years, I have had an incredible impact, almost like a grand awakening that swept through my body, with all the zigzagging of life and living much of my decisions independently. My truth has empowered every decision I have made and created connections with many people who have been guides along my journey.

I continue to find that love, in its deepest essence, is a spiritual experience. My journey within myself has been deeply personal; cultivating it has been unbelievably gratifying.

For my marriage and motherhood moving forward in my fifties, I have realized I will never be in the same place emotionally or spiritually with those in my life, which has been a critical component for me to understand. We can be on two separate paths but maintain a connection by communicating. I want to keep homing in on how to explore that symbiotic relationship between my journey and theirs, with the hope of uncovering a more intimate connection and becoming a catalyst for individual growth and healing.

My inner mirror, Dad, has given me some tremendous self-reflection. My interactions with others have revealed aspects of myself that I was not fully aware of, and maybe I chose to ignore.

Through conflict, misunderstanding, and soulful moments, each held up mirrors to my soul and reflected my strengths, weaknesses, and deepest desires.

My partner of twenty-six years has been there to uncover my deep capacity to be patient, forgive, and have compassion for him and me. I have tried to show up with an open heart in all our challenges. Much of what he has shown me is an unlearning.

love, me

Dear Dad,

You would be pleased. Every damn day, I keep learning to live, it's a little bit messy, but I am practicing civility, which has been gratifying. I recognize consideration for myself and others who may not have earned it.

As I have written, it has been hard to stay kindhearted when people have not been kind to me and those people have violated my value and worth. Did I allow them to? Is the question I keep pondering? All I know is right now, I keep deconstructing my discontent.

But I knew I needed clarity for years. I struggled with association and disassociation with those who do not deserve my goodness, nor that of my husband and children. Yet, teaching self-worth while not giving in to the monetary beast is a work in progress, whether in life with work or in a family whose love language is money. What I realized is it's not mine to control or monitor. How we each manage our relationships will be different with each individual.

The time it has taken for me to have a deep understanding of what has been happening here finally surfaced … here is the list in no specific order:

- I wanted more "love" from others than they could give.
- I felt attacked and/or abandoned, whether it was Mom, Martin, Tim, his father and stepmother, or Shiloh; learning how the safety of what I expected and felt was family or love was not supposed to treat me that way.
- I now recognize that their behaviors towards me were their discontent or wounds from their experiences.
- These people were not mine to fix, carry, or worry about.
- Letting people be who they are, unless there is a direct attack on me, which there were several, then act and defend accordingly.
- I had to give myself love but find it within first.

love, me

Dear Dad,

Turning fifty in April brought a mix of reflections and emotions to the surface. A milestone to reflect on being alive, how at thirty, like you, I was unsure how much time I had left. This number is also a reassessment of my future goals and really think about who and what truly matters and feels meaningful in my life.

Holding on tight to what I love and value is easy for me. Once I took time to work through my anger and resentment toward those I feel have wronged me, my eyes opened up to what anger really is. Together with resentment, hurt, sadness, and being let down in the relationships in my life have torn at the essence of my being. I want to move forward in life and love but not bringing the harm of others. All these emotions I listed showed me I care. I care for those in my life despite the actions I felt harmed me. My vulnerability in wanting more from them was a me problem, not a *them* problem.

It took time alone and doing the inner work to realize that valuing people properly makes a difference in the expectation I have of them and the relationships.

When you died, I longed for love. I wanted anything from anyone. Without receiving it, I turned and gave it to everyone around me. Mom was absent. Shiloh needed to be protected and cared for. Other family members were living their lives and unaware of the inner workings of our family and my feelings. Mom marries and this guy is not emotionally available, nor were the in-laws I desperately needed a second family from. My husband had love, but protected himself and was unable to give me what I needed, and our new family needed due to his childhood trauma. Well, that left a gaping hole in my heart to be filled.

I needed to take time to heal. Rationalizing my reasons for being angry was easy. As a recovering people pleaser, I wanted to solve problems. I had placed myself in confinement with the relentless unending cycle of all my relationships.

I kept aiming at something unattainable.

My anger was because I was betrayed, Dad. The relationships I had were fundamentally a broken dynamic with each operating on different realities. I knew what I needed, but those around me fell short of my standard and weren't playing by the same values. They didn't acknowledge wrongdoing and lacked the self-aware-ness or desire for self-transformation.

They refused to apologize when they wronged me. I was the only one stepping up and acknowledging when I could have done better. This may sound self-righteous, but it's how I feel and what has happened over time with many of those close to me.

As I stepped into a deeper understanding of self, I no longer place value on the relationship. I love and value me more. The desire to return to good terms is not a priority, and I have let go of my expectations and anger of those who were not there for me.

Tim and I have worked toward partnership and safety. I have voiced over many uncomfortable conversations my desire for someone who shows up for me and also works on themselves. It cannot just be one of us doing the heavy lifting in the relationship. As we take on new roles, he recognizes my silent suffering, and I recognize why he struggles to communicate. We want our mar-riage to be a space where we both, as flawed individuals, grow and evolve. I want a partner who can contribute, have difficult conver-sations, and show up as the best version of himself possible.

In the end, Dad, I just want transparency and a willingness to communicate and have empathy for each other. Relationships are about togetherness, just like family, together is better.

Tim and I have crossed the intersection of past pain from what transpired with his first family and mine. He knows I will not carry the emotional load of him his family or our family together and shutting me out will only exasperate the problem. We are true companions. We have been to rock bottom and secure enough in ourselves to work through times when we don't like what the other is doing. I want to be with someone who shows up when the fairy tale doesn't exist and is willing to do hard things. For me, openness to change, emotional maturity and accountability are my prince charming features.

The serendipity of life and its lessons still make me smile. I remind myself daily, I am more than I am allowing myself to be. Giving myself to be a beginner, time and time again.

love, me

Dear Dad,

I am officially fifty years old! While there have been a lot of dark times, there have been so many good times, too. I have grown so much in the last few years and have finally started making peace with my past and accepting that I can't continue to sacrifice my happiness for others. The relentless cycle of drama circulates around me, but I am not getting involved, Dad.

I cannot be everyone's strength anymore. I have been attacked too many times for protecting them.

For too long, I have tolerated the behaviors of many people who have not shown me light, only darkness.

Dad, I am finally saying *enough*.

After attending a women's workshop for four days in Santa Barbara with a group of eight dynamic dames who had been vulnerable with their struggles in life, understanding much is rooted in our first family. We all shared our journeys and connected in an open, inspiring environment with a girl guru I am interviewing for volume three of *S.H.E.* While our childhoods were different, we shared a common thread that led us to the happy places we are still creating. I feel fortunate to meet many women who share similar values and interests in learning to love oneself on the way back home. All the rest of our relationships that swirl and whirl around us are just noise.

Despite my continued state of not belonging within my first family and the family I married into, I have created a safe space within my nuclear family of Tim, Cole, and Cody. I will fight for their safety and our togetherness. I am not the target of attack by those three men, which is why I am happy to have them see me and love me for who I am. They don't use my strength against me; they encourage me to keep being me.

Far too long since your death, I stopped taking care of myself and started taking care of everyone around me. As I move forward into this new unknown, what I do know is I would rather my silence be misinterpreted than my words be misquoted, or my presence mishandled.

Learning the importance of being still and seeing me and allowing myself to be more than those around me, an acceptance of sorts, has been profound and offered great insight into the pain I have been feeling.

People only change when they want to.

As I continue to work on my inner self, I return to my greater inner divine and the angels you have sent to protect me, keeping me safe and sane. I know my hurt and tears over the years have not been wasted. They have been my fuel, giving me more and more confirmation of how my intuition has been my best friend.

I am grieving the little girl inside of me, that eleven-year-old who had her world turned upside down when her dad died. I finally found a way of letting go of learned behaviors that have saved me in the past. Speaking up for myself, defending loved ones, and holding everything together as the responsible one, was a heavy load that served me well then. Now, however, I don't want to be the accountable one all the time. I no longer want to live life for everyone else. The guilt of letting go of giving myself to others and putting that energy toward myself feels selfish, but I am gradually getting past it.

Here are some hard truths that I had to accept:

- I don't need to hold it all together.
- I don't need to do everything for everyone.
- I don't have to have it all figured out.
- I don't have to buy into the notion that hard work equals honor.
- I don't have to buy into being creative is not being productive.
- I don't believe that a corporate job will make me feel complete and have that sense of accomplishment.
- I can be soft and taken care of.
- I can reconcile resentment and anger by releasing what no longer serves me.
- My husband is not the enemy.
- My kids will be fine.

My journey back home was to me. A forever warm fuzzy feeling of love again, like I felt when I was young.

As I continue to take my broken parts of my existence and lovingly acknowledge the pain they have caused, and the lessons they taught, their power has made me whole again.

I know you hear me. I know you have been here guiding me in some form, Dad. A type of big fuck-you to the momentum of social constructs and human conditioning that one must stay in place to belong, well I remembered I belong to me. No matter how difficult and jarring life has been, I have found a release of how to leave dysfunctional relationships behind.

The "Dear Dad" diary of writing my inner feelings was not one of escape but of liberation. A type of pilgrimage to the heart of who I am beyond the facades and masks I wore for those around me as survival.

I wish we could have this conversation in person but thank you for offering me a sacred space of introspection within the solace of my solitude. I found wisdom in the silence and strength in the simplicity of our one-way exchange.

As I explore the inner landscape of me, a feeling of relationship release has taken place and I awakened my real self again, as an act of rebellion and liberation. You taught me this!

The journey through loss and loneliness led me back to loving myself. Thanks, Dad. I love you.

love, me

Dear Reader,

There has been so much silent work that I have been doing, and nobody ever knew the internalizing I was unraveling and trying to make sense of. It has been an actual grind; doing it without any applause or recognition except for myself has been the most rewarding. I did and continue to do it for me. As I continue to turn the pages of time, I am coming to understand what it means to let people be and let them fight and argue with themselves. The attacks on me I would personalize, but with time and therapy, I now recognize the poisonous darts at my heart were their attempt to defend their ego to feel safe with who they think they are. Nothing I say or do will change their mind, as they are correct, and the word reflection is not in their vocabulary except maybe how they appear in their mirrors. I know what's in my mirror looking back.

The idea that we all have these egos, and somehow, they become deeply attached to our self-image, does fascinate me. When I was taking several psychology courses back when the boys were in grade school, as I thought I wanted to be a marriage and family therapist, the perpetual fear of losing control kept all of us carefully constructing our identities. And when challenged, the ego somehow employs various defensive strategies to protect the narrative it created. How the brain does this is still being researched, but wow, was this excellent information to stumble upon during these times of confusion and chaos with family drama and dysfunctions that I was trying to sift through?

Within my marriage, it has taken time for me to no longer desperately fortify my walls and cling to this sense of sense that felt threatened. I wanted my husband to defend me, but in the end, I needed to understand why I was so angry with the actions against me by his father and even my husband. In those moments, as I reflect, I realize it was rarely about me, those moments of his father being critical, or my husband not taking my side against his father was me not always wanting to be the one fighting for me, for the injustice around me, I wanted my husband to handle, but all along their words and actions reflected not my flaws, or expectations of them both in a different manner but their fears and insecurities. His father needed to strengthen his self-image by belittling me, and my husband grew up in an environment that allowed a power imbalance and money as a means to maintain control as a form of love.

Far too many times, I attempted to step into their arena, defend myself, or make them and others around me understand. But engaging in their conflict, or lack thereof, was like trying to smooth out waves in the ocean—exhausting and ultimately futile. His father's actions and my husband's inaction felt like arrows aimed at my heart, but the truth was that I was not the target. I became caught in the crossfire and their internal battles, individually and collectively. I never really knew how to step back and take a deep breath.

Only now, I type this, do I finally see the words and actions "of others" as an echo of their inner turmoil, not my worth. I felt for most of my marriage, and while his father was alive, if I chose not to engage, I was admitting defeat. I would never run away from confrontation when someone wrongs me. But now, it is crystal clear I needed to recognize that some battles are not mine to fight. This also plays into the overall picture, including my mother and sister.

Now I am doing a much better job of preserving my energy for things that matter such as my growth, purpose, passions, peace, and joy, which include my two adult sons, but letting go of guiding and protecting them has been another hurdle, as they are now of age to do it themselves. I have become a living example or case study—you can't control how others perceive you, but you can choose how you respond. I embolden them to select self-respect. I encourage them to let others be who they are, knowing their journey is theirs, just as mine is mine.

My journey has been long but as I stand here now, looking back on my life, I have come to understand that we all have trauma, we all have nightmares, we all have pain. However, dear reader, how we choose to pick ourselves up and carry on is the only thing that matters in the end.

love, me

The Therapy Sessions
A Note from Tristen

Dear Reader,

The ease of middle-to-late-therapy is a well-deserved achievement. It may indicate fewer sessions, but the work is still intense with a much higher expectation of accountability. It requires years of deep emotional dives that reveal both treasures and carcasses on each journey to the metaphorical ocean floor.

Shannon understands the nature of these deep dives. She is no stranger to the dangers and rewards of self-work and self-healing.

Her healthy emotional processing, ability to recognize trauma triggers, avoid spiritual dangers and improve emotional regulation to allow for decoding the accurate source of trauma activation is impressive.

In the healing years, I no longer need to guide these deep explorations of self. The shifting from guide to observer increases with each session. Her fearlessness, her self-work in between sessions and having tough conversations with her partner has been fulfilling and insightful.

Her inner circle has been reworked as her boundaries and self-worth expanded. Her capacity for imperfection of self has evolved and her willingness to listen increased. Her interpersonal relationships are more layered, more satisfying, more purposeful, more meaningful, more congruent.

Very rarely do we need to confront unhealthy exchanges of energy or self-betrayal. And when we do, we know the reason, the right tool, and how the power of writing facilities her healing.

These improvements are the result of countless self-exploration efforts. A unique balance of alone time and human connection. An endless thirst for more knowing, more growth.

Perhaps the pinnacle of her life's work and the summation of healing her inner child is Mama Bear Shannon. A mother fiercely protecting, loving, and nurturing those beautiful humans—Cole and Cody. Putting them first, reparenting herself while parenting them, breaking dysfunctional generational cycles, guiding her family on the uncharted road of emotional intelligence has profoundly altered the course of this family system. She is a role model for all mothers who need their own healing.

I know her partner would never want any credit, but Tim does deserve the influential position of securest attachment. Years of witnessing, experiencing, and contributing to these layers of transformation. I thank you, Tim, for gifting her true unconditional love. I see you, TC!

There are countless other people, therapeutic tools, and experiences vital to her healing process. Many other contributors added to her selflove, softening, self-compassion, insight, and her ability to create healthier relational patterns.

Many other lessons remain untold yet impactful to her story.

Shannon, you have protected yourself and so many others. Your diligence has paid off. I know you will continue to stay true to who you are a person, trusting your Rosie. I am honored to be on this healing journey with you, my tenacious friend. Forever and always.

xoxo
Love, Tristen

The Resentment Session
by Tristen

I log into my Telehealth software and click on the session link revealing Shannon, who is already smiling brilliantly, ready to work. I am six minutes late.

"What is on your heart today?" I ask.

"My marriage," she responds. "I want more. This pacing thing is exhausting." She sighs as she pulls a pair of glasses off her head. "I'm just waiting for the part where we deep dive and level up together."

"I want to take a moment to honor where we've been and where we are," I say. "Both of you have been committed to healing generational trauma and patterns."

"I feel like I need to get out of here," she states flatly.

"This sounds like compassion fatigue, Shannon. You are tired of holding space for your partner's timing. What you see as restless, I see as anxious-avoidant attachment. Losing your father deeply impacted the secure attachments in your life. Not only did you lose your father, but your mother pulled into herself. Both losses caused significant emotional neglect in the family system. Truly a double abandonment.

"When we are impacted by loss so young, it creates intense uncertainty. Anyone, at any age, would feel disoriented. Especially a teenager, with an underdeveloped brain, carrying the

251

heavy burden of keeping a pulse on her little sister's and mother's needs," I say.

We both know the story well.

"Your response to abandonment was age appropriate," I continue. "You learned to cope with abandonment by wandering, escaping into books, riding your bike aimlessly, journaling, becoming intensely familiar with aloneness. Pulling inward created safety for you. You taught yourself how to be comfortable alone. You taught yourself to avoid closeness, to avoid being let down. In order to heal the abandonment wounding you will need to create more secure attachments. Healing happens in connection, Shannon. I want you to practice reassuring yourself with these affirmations: *I am capable of authentic connection. I am worthy of secure, healthy attachments. I am safe as I learn to share my inner world with those I trust.*"

"Your abusers are powerful teachers," I say. "They have been influential mirrors revealing your people-pleasing tendencies and highlighting poor boundaries. It is okay for pain to swirl back through your system. It's a process for trauma activation to inform you of what feels familiar, to protect yourself from walking back into the same damaging patterns. But you need to hold yourself accountable for this. You cannot punish your partner for his pacing," I warn.

"We will honor your partner's pacing. The journey is just as difficult and as painful for each of you. Continue to learn who your partner actually *is*—stop telling him who he needs to be. This only promotes defensiveness and pushes you further apart."

She shares intimate details of their communication, her need for space, his confusion about what she wants from him.

I guide us through a compassion fatigue exercise.

What is getting in the way of accepting your partner for who he is?
What's getting in the way of you seeing little Tim?

With his own wounds and his own unmet needs and his own heart aches?

"The only way to deepen your marriage connection," I say, "is to learn a new way of communicating. *Listen* to his words and think about how to stay curious about what is under the surface," I encourage.

What does his behavior indicate he needs? How does he respond to your feedback? Are you telling him who to be or are you trying to understand who he is ? How is his behavior protecting him?

And what is your part in all this?

What are you truly trying to tell Tim?

Are you teaching him the why?

"It is considered a hidden agenda until you say it out loud, Shannon." "But he should know."

"Tell him what you need," I push. "Tell him what you desire. Tell him in detail what will help you feel more connected to him in this moment. Not one of the men in your past tried even half as much as your own husband to understand you, to believe you, to honor your experiences. Don't punish the one person willing to see you and fully accept you for who you are. Let him be your safe space. He deserves a partner who loves him unconditionally, just as much as you do."

She knows. She sees the impasse. She's never been afraid to hear the truth. "I will throw myself into another project. I will not self-destruct."

We both appreciate that she can handle this raw, blunt feedback. It takes tremendous courage to see our part in a marriage. It takes great perseverance to stay in the stuckness and trust more growth is possible. It takes intense vulnerability to sync up life goals and dreams for decades.

Staying married is not for the faint of heart.

This is not your typical marriage. This marriage is remarkably complex and incredibly special. This marriage is worth fighting for.

The Divorce Session
by *Tristen*

The tension is palpable. My gaze darts back and forth between them, searching for nonverbal clues. They strain smiles through clenched teeth and shallow breathing. They are sitting on opposite ends of the couch, arms folded. Today is not a day for pleasantries. I jump right in.

"What is happening?" I ask.

They both look at one another and back at me. We are all blinking and scanning each other's face.

"Well, it might be time," Shannon says shifting in her seat. "Time to talk about divorce."

"*What?*" I yell. "What are you talking about?"

"I don't know if we can get past this one," Tim agrees.

They detail the deadlock. I only see two small, scared children on my couch. A small young Shannon and a small young Tim. Two wounded souls trying to find their way in this wounded world.

"Divorce needs to be off the table," I implore. "I need you to hear me out. Neither of you needs another attachment injury, that is for damn sure. Your sons don't need more distance between their parents. They need two imperfect people to work it out. Divorce is trading in '*these problems*' for '*these problems*'," I say with both of my hands out, palms up like the scales of justice. "What

I mean, is that instead of the problems of the marriage you are getting the problems of the divorce—coparenting in two different households, blended families, hostile exchanges as we pass off the kids, loneliness when apart from your kids, financial changes, chronic resentment."

They stare at me.

"Both sets of problems aren't improved apart," I continue. "The issues are draining and certainly impact feeling safe and close in this family system. You both have had a front row seat to this with your own parents. Divorce doesn't fix any of these challenges and living in separate dwellings or dating the next person doesn't change that you are forever tied to each other by your children! Every birthday, every milestone, weddings, funerals, celebrations, even future grandchild's moment requires you both to be mature, respectful, co-existers who prioritize your sons' needs over your own comfort. That is what divorce requires," I say. "That means you both better squeeze every ounce of self-examination about how you can improve this marriage and learn to soothe yourself when your childhood wounds are activated. There is no loophole, no secret key under a secret rock in a secret forest. There is only self-exploration, self-awareness and self-improvement. It's the only way through." Two hurt, wounded souls stare back at me.

It is a good day to save a marriage.

"Higher level consciousness in a marriage means hanging in there during conflict. It means tolerating the tension in a power struggle and striving to deeply understand the process within you and within your partner. Saying the *D-word*, even casually, is creating an exit. I caution you both about this destructive cycle. Feeling justified in belittling or blaming our pain is only making you more unsafe for your partner. Honest conversations are hard enough, hearing hyper critical language and airing grievances that have been discussed, reviewed, understood, and resolved the best way they can be, has to be enough."

I focus on Shannon. "You need to stop punishing people for what you also participated in. You must exercise more restraint in this area. Threatening divorce communicates your pain, but it certainly isn't improving anything. It is signaling that your abandonment wounding needs more soothing. You are also triggering your partner's own abandonment wounds, making it impossible for a healthy, fair conflict. Your partner has owned his part in your pain. He has admitted to the ways he contributed to your hurt. He has shifted at your urging. He has expanded at your insistence. He has thrown himself into the messy and complicated world of self-healing. He has changed. This is exactly what you hoped for and dreamed about in your marriage relationship. You cannot move the finish line. You do not get to minimize his efforts. I will tell him the exact same thing," I insist.

I focus on him.

"Tim, you will not take this lightly. You will not promise to dive into the sea of intimacy and take more days off than you work at it. Your partner is imploring you to stretch, expand, and grow. You will continue to find ways to reveal more insights and layers of yourself. You airing out incongruences doesn't promote connection or safety. It promotes hostility and misunderstanding. Her promoting self-awareness is exhausting to follow, well, imagine if you had to lead like she is. You will not give up when your hard work is just beginning to become more natural. Your sons are watching. They are looking to you to lead this family, to show them what a vulnerable, adult man looks like. I will not let you pull out of this marriage because of either one of you acting out. This is called leveling up. This is what we have been working toward. No way we give up now!"

The room goes quiet. The weight of this moment is thundering in our ears. One of their phones barely vibrates and no one even thinks to reach for it. I can feel my intensity.

"I am not here to heal you, Shannon. I am not here to heal you, Tim. *You* will heal yourselves."

I stop for several long minutes. All of us reflective and serious.

"I want to analyze this in a practical way. Shannon, you feel angry and resentful toward your partner and say, 'You never stood up for me! You should have protected me!' He is now activated in his own stress response unsure of how to soothe you or soothe himself. He says, 'I have apologized and taken responsibility for my part. I have promised to do better going forward and proven that I can. I will continue to do better.' You feel far apart because you are not revealing your true, deep pain. Are we projecting, Shannon? Are we punishing Tim for his offenses, or the offenses of another?" I inquire.

"Are we projecting, Tim?" I ask him. "Are we punishing Shannon for her offenses, or the offenses of another? Do you resent her for pushing you? Both of you must stop recycling trust injuries when you feel tremendous hauntings from the past. Both of you are fighting demons of dysfunction, childhood wounds, and reconciling your self-betrayals. Stop injuring the progress by being too harsh. Stop punishing *him* for a process you are both barely beginning to understand your parts in. Stop punishing *her* for needing to create understanding of her story.

This is dangerous territory.

"Your roles are to honor the intensity of these feelings. Honor your part in the process. He is imperfect." I point to Tim. "She is imperfect." I point to Shannon. "No one here is an expert on anything other than themselves. So, each of you, take accountability for your rage, your hurt, your pain, your projecting. Annihilating your partner doesn't heal your hurt from any of the others who hurt either one of you. We are *not* doing this!" I declare.

They both look relieved.

They both want the marriage to work.

They both can and will do better.

The Father Wound Session
by Tristen

"Upon reflection of my intense journaling homework, Shannon says, "I notice another layer of childhood wounding. I deeply long for a father figure. I unconsciously created a dynamic of longing for my father-in-law to be that."

At first glance, he was an excellent candidate. He appeared capable, interested, and imperfect which likely made me feel like it was possible. The more I pour myself into him, the more depleted I feel.

I now see I created an unhealthy cycle of assuming he is capable of loving me unconditionally and now recognizing that it was transactional at best for him.

"What is painful to admit," she says, "is that I've pulled Tim into this father figure role. I have tried to guide us both into what a healthy, loving father looks like. Now I see I keep taking on projects that were never mine to begin with," she insightfully explains.

"Ask yourself: is this constructive or could this be a projection?" I say. "Is this helpful or do I have a hidden agenda? A better way to share how you experience your feelings is to use an 'I feel statement.' For example, *I feel the distance between us, and I want to bring it up as soon as I notice it so we can look at it together.* This is a healthier communication style. It allows the listener to stay present and hear your words rather than scrambling to defend himself or promote judgements."

"Okay, I'm ready to practice," she says. "Tim, I felt unsupported at dinner with your family. Your dad cracked 'jokes' that were cruel comments about me, and when I directly addressed this, they were dismissed as banter. When I am catering to the needs of others, I am in self-betrayal. I am bustling around the room, pouring my energy into each of the emotionally disabled adults. I created this pattern in the family system to fit in," she says without hesitation.

"Flawless," I respond.

Shannon continues, "Now I know better. I am now conscious that these interactions leave me feeling depleted and unseen. I realize now it is painful for me, because it is effort unreceived. I created this version of me who spends family gatherings attending to the needs of others, prioritizing their preferences and wants while betraying my own comfort." "Keep going," I urge.

"When I turn to you for comfort, I am met with an avoidant version of you. I feel hurt that you didn't stand up for me. I feel angry and resentful toward you, him, and myself for this pattern," she determines.

"It's happening," I declare with a smile. "You are healing!"

She doesn't miss a beat. "This is a reenactment of a pattern omnipresent in my childhood. My deepest childhood wound. I desperately needed my mom to see me, to walk away from dysfunction and violence. Her decision to be stoic and detached impacted me by creating a deep longing to be seen," she states with conviction. I am floored. "Impressive, Shannon. Truly impressive." She smiles brightly.

"Our best healing is intertwined with our interpersonal relationships," I explain. "Our relationships reveal where we have more room to grow. We have an opportunity to take this information and expand. Consider it like trimming the fat. Digest the bulk of the message and let the rest of it go. To heal from trauma, we must learn how to trust ourselves again, return to our bodies, and forgive ourselves for what we did while we were in survival mode."

"This is self-love. This is you, Shannon. This is your story."

Numbville

by Shannon

Reclaiming my life was not a mess to be disentangled, but an unknown journey to be lived.

For years I have secretly dreamed of becoming a creative writer, playwright, or even poet. An educationalist who enjoys using stories to motivate and illuminate the movements of others.

In childhood, my shortcomings were presented to me as inexcusable actions. Never once did my elders explain my misadventures could be used as guides. If I was disrespectful, they would use verbal threats, house arrest, and my ultimate favorite—washing out my mouth with soap. These scare tactics were implemented during the era of *children are to be seen and not heard*, which was a difficult motto for me to adhere to. As I matured, I realized this instruction was poor advice. I discovered my missteps were my story poles, a way to construct my dreams.

Early in my elementary years, my sister and I would frequently play school in our basement. She was always considerate each time I demanded to be the teacher. It was during these times of role playing that I surprised myself and began practicing my own make-believe instructions for life and learning. There was an inner representative tucked inside telling me these wrong turns and errors made would not impact my ability for success but serve as guideposts to the aspirations I had yet to uncover.

There was certainly no talk of dreams or desires in my family. That would have been on the verge of a fantasyland where unicorns and pixie dust coexist! Nevertheless, my sister and I would carry on with our imaginary games. But reality always slipped in and stole our fantasies making our mistakes front and center again. My inside representative reminded me that my voice and feelings mattered; it was up to me to create a space for both.

During my teens, I experienced my inner representative repeatedly offering advice. Oftentimes, it would challenge my own and others' reasoning. This instinctive feeling reminded me to confront myself. It wanted me to question the obvious and the norms presented to me. Was this inner representative a spirit telling me right from wrong? People questioned my stability and felt my strange ways needed additional correction. There was never any proof this inner representative existed, but it was such a strong feeling that it still resonates with me today.

At the time, it seemed logical to name this sensation. She felt like my inner goddess, a guiding light or, better yet, a woman warrior. I named her Rosie. She seemed to be the only person who really understood my idiosyncrasies. As the years passed, this inner representative, which could possibly be called my intuition, had plenty of things to tell me. It took an absurd amount of time for me to listen.

My internal, gutsy spirit Rosie reminded me how I had gone astray and directed me to change course many times in my life.

Living is drama, get used to it.

The realization that most things are not what they seem isn't something you want to learn at the age of eleven. Although you knew the life and death cycle occurred around you naturally, you were abruptly awakened to this force when your thirty-year-old, adored father had to die. This is when your initiation into life began. Life moved you rather quickly from the fur-lined nest of what you believed to be "normal" to the jolting jungle of your new environment.

She was animated and had a way with words. This vibrant dame understood that my life experiences brought with them complex and confusing roles, and she had a deliberate process of guiding me through these times.

Rosie became a trusted friend and confidante.

Stop allowing fractured, missing pieces of bliss dim your light.

You need to fix your fragmented mess. You allowed yourself to be compromised. Find answers. Go and locate a place within yourself where you can find refuge.

Huh?

Did she want me to address my pain?

Solve past problems?

How does that work?

When does one start?

Where does one locate this place of protection within?

It was an overwhelming task, and I was not ready to exert the effort and "feel" all my painful feelings in order to find inner contentment. There was too much awareness necessary to complete this task. It was far easier to submerge my past negative experiences and frustrations.

We officially lost communication.

It was in this moment of feeling alone that I began plotting my path to avoidance. My sanctuary was in clear sight. I began my escape from childhood pain and situated myself within my own inner, fictional town of refuge.

Welcome to Numbville.

A place where people wind up when they give up.

Countless visitors yearly.

Hometown to many.

Population unknown.

Feel free to come and go as you please.

I entered Numbville in hopes of finding solace from my imbalanced feelings. Each person I encountered seemed to lack the zest for life. Many appeared bitter. Others looked sad.

Many were emotionally misplaced, like me.

All occupants looked numb. Most looked victimized.

Here in front of me were numerous folks who had been abused, used and undervalued. Several were abandoned, ignored and bullied.

Countless citizens had a combination of all the above.

I felt disoriented. Why had I ignored my inner woman warrior? Do I even belong here?

"Misery loves company," the town mayor expressed upon my arrival. He seemed like a charismatic fellow—a divorced dad of three girls. He went on to say, "Many of our long-term tenants wanted to feel free and ignore the unhappiness which brought them to this secluded safe haven." He shared with me that his wife and girls do not live here, nor do they visit.

Periodically, he will visit them. However, feeling vulnerable outside this walled city he calls home is not for him.

"We stuff our former disappointments and drama into a deep, dysfunctional cistern when we arrive, and there they stay," shared the local diner waitress who had been psychologically and physically maltreated by all the men in her life. "It is a ceremonious celebration every time we get a new resident. In fact, the local gambler constantly takes bets around town, if this newbie will be a lifer or not." I was speechless.

The town was devised to keep you dazed and delirious.

How can they help me? Or, better yet, how can I help myself?

These questions must have agitated Rosie, I could feel her sweltering sense wanting to scream at me. She finally snapped, *These people are just going through the motions of life! There is no meaning or understanding in their lives. What these individuals are missing is the deeper experience of it. They fell victim to their tank of troubles.*

I was deeply confused and conflicted. I longed for answers.

Town gossip and recovering alcoholic Ms. Gizzie was ready to lend a hand. She indicated that, "No one really leaves once they begin to take comfort in the ordinary." It seemed logical, since Numbville was never designed to be lively, but to help people find comfort in the discomfort.

Gizzie introduced me to the sheriff, a diagnosed narcissist who continues to struggle with his passive aggression. He pointed out with a devious grin, "It's the can-do, crazy ones who try to retrieve their tragedies from the cistern and leave. It can be challenging. We attempt to distract them, but the strong-willed ones bolt—never establishing permanent residency."

I sensed Rosie was impatient with me. She found me chatting with Gizzie, who was providing a sort of nirvana from the turbulent times my outside world was doling out.

Rosie suddenly pronounced, *Being neglected emotionally and physically was not fun for you. It led you to being expressively empty and unavailable for most of your young adulthood. You were internally disordered and disenchanted with your life. This is why you drifted from me and found sanctuary in this fictional town you have generated.*

It was this brief reminder along with her powerful insight about my past that told me I did not belong here. It had been years since I took her advice, and it was time to experience life again. No more submerging my past negative experiences and frustrations!

Yes, the highs and lows of my life felt overwhelming. The idea of finding a place to take shelter from the constant confusion seemed logical. The inside and outside noises around me dulled when I was in my place of refuge. No one bothered me here in Numbville. I would watch the world and all its players like a variety show. There was limited participation, and it was half-hearted—like never being fully alive in my own body. I found comfort, safety, and security staying within the confines of this walled city.

As I slowly regained consciousness, Rosie demanded, *You need to revitalize me. Slowly, reshape your world back into reality.*

Quickly, I realized these citizens and this community were not interested in personal growth or self-reflection. Introspection was blasphemy. Evolution was a crime. My short-lived visit made me realize I needed to flee.

It was at this juncture that Rosie consoled me, *You need to stop living in Numbville. Stop hiding. No more wallowing. You are not alone. There are others in the real world, like you, who have built their own imaginary towns.*

Was she serious? Are there others who have built similar towns within themselves?

I need to find them. Maybe we can help each other out?

Oh, Wait....

Dear Dad & Reader,

I thought I would end this with one last letter—to both of you.

To the man whose absence shaped my life, and to the ones holding these pages, wondering if their own story might find peace, too.

I thought these diary entries would be my final fight song—a bold and brave push against all the ways I felt silenced. But now I see it more clearly. These were never meant to be my fight songs; they were love songs.

To you, *Dad*. To the parts of me I lost and found again. To the memories that never left, and to the girl and woman who longed for someone to protect her, and became that someone, finally, for herself. I used to believe I needed to explain the family dynamics that broke me, how I tried to fix them, and how I was cast as the problem for naming what others kept sweeping under the rug. The years I wore roles I never asked for — peace-keeper, protector, performer, and fixer — were carried on for far too long, especially in family systems built on maintaining dishonest harmony rather than honest conflict. I learned it's the truth-teller who often gets cast as the challenging one. What I know now: I am not the problem. I am the pattern-breaker. And most importantly, I no longer feel the need to explain myself to anyone but me.

And to you, *Reader*. My life review was never about blame or bitterness – it was only about honesty. My healing only happened when I stopped pretending the pain did not happen. I did not write this book to hurt anyone; I wrote it to stop hurting myself through the silence, which protected dysfunction and the silence that emotionally suffocated and buried me beneath layers of loyalty to people who could not meet me in truth.

My greatest heartbreak was not in the actions of others. It was in those moments that I betrayed my inner Rosie to keep the dishonest harmony. But peace that costs your voice is not peace, it's performance. Coming home to yourself is the fiercest act of love. And speaking your reality, even when those around you would rather you stay silent, is something worth fighting for.

So, to anyone who has felt unseen in their own family, unheard in their truth, or unworthy of the kind of love that does not require shrinking – I see you. I see your courage and clarity. I see myself now, too, and learned this the long, hard way: *you don't have to bury the truth just because others can't bear to look at it – maintain your integrity, resilience, and independence of thought even if you need to stand alone.*

Breaking generational patterns is not for the faint of heart. It requires courage, clarity, and the audacity to face what is considered challenging, awkward, and name the problem. It also means choosing truth over comfort, boundaries over blind loyalty, and healing over habit. I am no longer the one who protects others at the expense of my peace, while wanting my mom and others to shield me, to step in, to say, "This isn't your burden to carry." But they never did. And in time, I realized I didn't need them to anymore. I needed me!

So here I am—a woman no longer performing and no longer pretending. Just living. And telling my truth. These forty years of diary entries are not wrapped in a tidy bow; instead, they are layered, raw, and human, accompanied by insights from Tristen, my trusted therapist. I feel invigorated having healed myself from things that were not my fault, holding that little Shannon and reminding her I am her defender now.

Thank you for bearing witness, and if you've ever been blamed for simply being honest... if you've ever been told you were too much, when you were just being real and raw – and uniquely you... if you've ever felt lonely and longed for someone to defend you and instead had to learn to defend yourself... this love song is for you, too.

This chapter in my life's book ends not with bitterness, but with *bravery*. Not with shame, but with *sovereignty*. Not with silence, but with *song*.

With love and liberation,
Me

About the Authors

Shannon Hogan Cohen writes to make sense of the world. From a young age, she filled notebooks with reflections, always searching for meaning, connection, and the hidden threads beneath life's surface, an instinct shaped by her childhood love of Nancy Drew mysteries. Whether it's finding patterns in chaos or truth in tangled relationships, storytelling has always been her compass.

A freelance writer with work published across community advocacy platforms, travel magazines, and personal essay outlets, Shannon gives voice to the often unspoken. She writes with heart, humor, and an unapologetic splash of truth-telling. When she's not wandering the world and championing legacies, you'll find her in her beloved "babe cave," savoring quiet moments of reading, writing, and sipping a cup of coffee or crisp white wine. She lives with her family in Del Mar, California.

Tristen Vance Henderson, MS, LMFT, developed a passion for working with children, adolescents, couples and families in community-based settings, inpatient and outpatient treatment, multiple schools, athletic, and corporate programs. She is an expert in the areas of trauma, sports psychology, interpersonal relationships, neurobiology, family systems, and clinical areas of PTSD, ADHD, and Anxiety / Depression.

Tristen is an Owner at Mission Oaks Counseling & Wellness Center, a center for healing that provides the tools for revitalization of the mind, body, and spirit. When she isn't saving the world or working on her own self-healing, Tristen recharges by spending time at the beach, reading, hiking, catching up with friends & family, and cheering for the Dodgers. She values her most important roles in life as Mama to her beautiful, sporty kids and Boxer, Sugar; Auntie T to her nieces, nephews and family of choice, and of course, most importantly, wifey to Cam.

www.ingramcontent.com/pod-product-compliance
Lightning Source LLC
Chambersburg PA
CBHW021710120626
46545CB00004B/1491